MW01052695

COMPETITION BBQ SECRETS

A barbecue instruction manual for serious competitors and back yard cooks too.

By
Bill Anderson

Copyright © 2008 Bill Anderson
All rights reserved.

ISBN: 1-4392-0911-1
ISBN-13: 9781439209110

Visit www.booksurge.com to order additional copies..

TABLE OF CONTENTS

INTRODUCTION

Dear Friend:

So you want to know how to barbecue? Well...you've picked the right book. Most barbecue books spend more time talking about grilling and they don't have a clue how to make good barbecue. We ain't gonna waste your time with grilling. Comparing grilling to slow-cooked barbecue is like trying to compare painting a house to painting a masterpiece of art. Any idiot can paint a house, but it takes skill, experience, and a love of art to create a true masterpiece. Cooking authentic, slow-smoked barbecue is what this book is all about. You're not gonna get the first side dish, dessert, or appetizer recipe here! Instead you will be taken step-by-step through the process of cooking mouth-watering "oh my God, that's good" barbecue.

When we first decided to try our luck in some BBQ competitions, I can't tell you how hard it was to find good information on preparing competition-quality meats. By the way..."competition quality" means BETTER than you will get in any restaurant. We bought books, videos, and scoured the Internet looking for help. What we found was that most sources of information left out the important details like cooking time and temperature. One-hundred-page books contained seventy-five pages of useless recipes. Videos left out the all-important details of time and temperature. Basically...we had to learn the hard way—through trial and error and gathering tips here and there from the pros. We wasted a lot of time and money and created a lot of "jerky." This book was written to help you avoid what we went through.

In the book, we will give a brief description of the different types of smokers available and the pluses and minuses of each cooker. It's up to you to decide what you want to cook on. Regardless of what you choose, the general process of cooking will be the same. A good barbecue cook can make good Q on everything from a $10,000 cooker to a hole in the ground. Once you learn how to master regulating temperature, you can cook good Q on anything.

Obviously, by buying this book you already have an interest in barbecue. We are not going to waste time and paper telling you the definition of the word "barbecue" or "barbeque" or "BBQ." WHO CARES where the word came from or what Mr. Webster thinks barbecue means? The only way to know the definition is to learn how to do it and then eat it! When you make the best barbecue you have ever eaten there won't be words to describe the way you feel. And when others eat your barbecue and they don't have words to describe how good it is— other than making caveman-like grunting noises—you'll know what barbecue means.

Let's not waste any more time...Read this book and then start your journey toward perfect Q!

Sincerely,
Bill Anderson

COOKERS

OFFSET SMOKERS

Offset smokers are by far the most popular type of cooker in BBQ competitions. They are easily recognized by the firebox on the side and not directly under the meat. You can buy small offset smokers at your local Home Depot or Bass Pro Shop or even Wal-Mart for around $100. These are good for beginners, but the firebox is small and it's hard to maintain a good fire without constant attention— and that can get tiresome after six to eight hours. Note: do not buy one of those really small offset smokers. They are a waste of money and are really hard to use. The minimum I would suggest is something like a Char-Broil Silver for $150 at Home Depot. The bigger smokers that look like they are made out of a propane tank start around $1,400 and go up from there. They have much bigger fireboxes and large grates that hold a lot of meat.

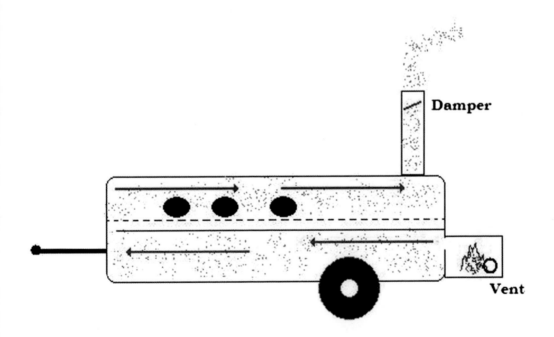

Take a look at the diagram...note how the smoke and heat travel under a solid metal plate all the way to the end of the smoker, go up to where the meat is located, and then out the chimney which is on the same side as the firebox. This is a nice feature that will give you a more even temperature under and around your meat. The heated metal plate helps maintain an even, constant temperature. Also note the vents and damper, which you will use to maintain your fire for proper temperature. This is just one design that is used by Lang smokers. Other offset-style smokers have the firebox on one end and the chimney on the other. Obviously, one end might get hotter than the other, so you'll have to "be prepared." Maybe put your chicken on the hotter end or make sure you rotate your meat often. It's important to understand your smoker and where the "hot spots" are so you don't cook at too high or low a temperature. Speaking of temperatures... make sure you measure your cooking chamber temperature "at the grate" where the meat is. Those thermometers in smokers' lids are usually 100°F off either high or low. A good thermometer is the Maverick dual probe remote thermometer, which has a probe for your cooking chamber temperature and a meat probe. You can get them at www.bbq-book.biz.

KETTLE GRILLS

Just about everybody has a Weber kettle charcoal grill in their backyard. You can smoke some pretty good ribs on these things. Here's how to set it up so that you are "offset smoking" and not grilling...first, light one charcoal chimney of coals without using lighter fluid. Once your coals are white, pour half of them in a small pile on one side of the grill and the rest in a small pile on the other side of the grill. Make sure your vents on the bottom of the grill are open and not clogged with ashes. Start soaking your wood chips at least an hour before you will need them. You can place a disposable aluminum pan between your charcoal piles and fill it with about an inch of warm water, or beer, if you want. When you are ready to start smoking, place your grate on the grill so that the holes near the handles are over your charcoal piles. This way, you can add charcoal as needed to maintain your heat. Some newer models have hinged grates for this purpose.

Now all you do is place your meat in the center of the grate—away from the charcoal piles. When I smoke ribs, I use a rib rack on top of the grate. Throw some soaked mesquite chips directly on the charcoal and close the lid (don't overdo the mesquite chips—mesquite imparts a strong smoke taste so a little goes a long way). Open the vents on the lid all the way and align the vents over your meat so the smoke will be drawn up and over your meat. Insert a thermometer through one of the vent holes. This is important! I use one of those confection/deep fry-style thermometers with the clip and long stem on it. You can also use a Maverick dual probe remote thermometer if you want. Make sure the probe wires are not draped directly over the coals or they will melt. It's important to measure the temperature as close to the meat as possible. Smoke your meat according to the directions found elsewhere in this book and you're all set! When the temperature gets too low, just open the lid and toss in a few new briquettes and/or soaked wood chips. Try to stay "ahead of the game" as far as heat is concerned because it's easier to cool down a hot smoker than it is to get it back up to temperature if your fire goes out.

VERTICAL SMOKERS

I used to own one of those Coleman propane smokers...that thing would smoke some succulent ribs! It was convenient too since all you had to do was throw some soaked wood chips on the lava rocks every now and then. Several other manufacturers like Brinkman and Weber make them too. They are all characterized by a heat source in the bottom and usually a water pan above that and then two or three levels of grates where you place your meat for smoking. They can be propane, charcoal/wood, or even electric. They are very easy to use and that water pan right above the heat source and then the meat placed directly above the water just seems to produce smoked meats that are more juicy and tender. It's hard to dry out your meats when they are constantly basted with moist heat. The water vapor is also a heat transport mechanism which helps maintain a constant temperature—I'm no scientist, but since water boils at 212°F, the water pan can't get any hotter than 212°. The excess heat is transported in the water vapor. That's real close to an ideal smoking temperature. Don't misunderstand me...your cooking chamber can still get hotter than 212°, but the water pan just helps to "regulate" your temperature. Some of the experts say that if your meat does not exceed 212°, then the juices in the meat don't evaporate—they just stay in and on the meat—effectively basting the meat in its own juices. But like I said...I'm no scientist!

THE COOKSHACK FAST EDDY 100 (FEC100)

I want to tell you about one of the best smokers on the market. But, in order to do that, I need to give you a little background into one of the best barbecue pitmasters of all time...a guy named Fast Eddy Maurin. Maybe he got that name from his off-road and midget car racing days—I don't know for sure. In addition to being a Kansas City, MO firefighter for many years, he has a great love of barbecue.

Fast Eddy Maurin has done very well on the competition barbecue circuit. In addition to numerous smaller barbecue competition grand championships, Fast Eddy was the 1998 Jack Daniels Reserve Grand Champion, the 1999 KCBS 4th overall team, 1998 World Pork Expo Champion, 1995 World Pork Expo winner of the pork shoulder category, and in 2000 Fast Eddy won the World Barbecue International Contest Ribs category with a perfect score. Now, I can tell you that is some accomplishment!

Sometime around 1998, Fast Eddy started manufacturing his own barbecue smokers using the skills he learned from his Dad in their fabrication shop. In 2002 Fast Eddy hooked up with Cookshack to manufacture his BBQ smokers for him. And that's how the FEC (Fast Eddy Cookers) line of barbecue smokers was born.

The FEC100 is the most popular Cookshack barbecue smoker on the competition circuit. The "100" stands for the amount of meat it will hold in

pounds. As a matter of fact, two of the last 3 year's Grand Championship winners at the Jack Daniels Invitational cooked on FEC100's.

Cookshack also has larger models including the FEC300, FEC500, and FEC750. Each can be purchased with or without a rotisserie. One cool thing that is fairly new with the Fast Eddy barbecue smokers is the new IQ4 controller. This is the standard controller that Cookshack has been using on their commercial barbecue smokers for a while. It is a *"cook and hold by probe"* controller. What this means is you can set a cooking chamber temperature and you can set a meat thermometer probe temperature. When the probe reaches a certain internal meat temperature, the controller will go into a holding pattern at a preset temperature which can be higher or lower than your cooking temperature and down to as low as 140°F. The controller will maintain the Fast Eddy cooking chamber temperature to within +-5°F.

When you are looking for a smoker, you should be looking for one that has lots of space, is easy to use, has consistent temperatures with no hot spots, is well insulated, is relatively low cost, and has a proven track record in winning contests. Very few barbecue smokers have all of these features.

Of course, if you didn't know it already, the Fast Eddy barbecue smokers are pellet smokers, so they are very easy to operate on those long overnight smokes. And if Fast Eddy Maurin says that pellets are better than real wood, you better take what he says seriously or you may just find yourself sitting in your chair while you watch someone else with a FEC100 walk across the stage to pick up their trophies! For full specifications and purchase information, visit www.bbq-book.biz

INSULATED AND CERAMIC SMOKERS

These types of smokers are a variation of the vertical smoker. Stump's and the Big Green Egg are two of the most popular manufacturers. The Stump's smoker is a vertical box shape and you can probably guess how the Big Green Egg is shaped. The walls of these smokers are very well insulated. They are great because you can put one bag of charcoal in the bottom of an insulated smoker and it will last about sixteen hours on one bag! That's a whole lot easier than checking your firebox every fifteen to thirty minutes! Stump's even has a new model with a gravity-fed charcoal system...as the charcoal burns, it makes way for more charcoal to automatically drop in from the feeder bin. With other types of smokers, you lose a lot of heat when you open the lid. With these types of smokers, more heat is maintained in the walls. You know what they say..."*If you're lookin', you ain't cookin'!*"

Stumps Smoker
←

Big Green Egg
→

SMOKING ON YOUR PROPANE GRILL

If you don't have a Weber kettle grill in your backyard, then you probably have one of these. They are mostly used for grilling—not slow smoking. But...if you have a two-burner model, you can slow smoke meats. Just use one burner on low or medium and put your meat on the other side of the grill—don't put your meat directly over the burner. This way, you can simulate an offset smoker. Here's a little trick to produce some pretty good smoke...wrap your wood chips or pellets tightly in some aluminum foil and then poke some holes in the top. Throw this packet directly on the lava rocks over the working burner. You can also buy little steel boxes made for this purpose. A water pan placed on the grate over the working burner would not be a bad idea either. Your meat will probably dry out faster with this "rig," but it's workable. Of course...keep an eye on your temperature *"at the grate"* and follow all the other directions on how to smoke meat found elsewhere in this book.

THE PIT

If you have a few extra "fire bricks" laying around, you can make a simple pit with three walls and a grate thrown over the top. A whole lot of BBQ restaurants use this method on a larger scale. Usually they have a separate fire that they maintain just for producing coals for the pit. They shovel the coals from the fire to the pit as needed. Don't get your meat too close to the coals or fire or you'll end up grilling instead of slow smoking. I've also seen some restaurants throw a big sheet of aluminum over the top of their meat to help keep the heat in. It's not pretty, but it's cheap and it works!

Here are some pictures of some fancy smokers at the Best of the Best BBQ Competition in Douglas, Georgia...

This smoker was featured on a Food Channel special...

TYPES OF WOOD

Have you ever been to a great barbecue restaurant and just stood outside and inhaled that wonderful smoke billowing from a wood-fired, brick pit? There is just something special about how barbecue smells as it slow cooks for hours upon hours. Let's get to work now on trying to duplicate that same aroma in your own smoker.

Most restaurant BBQ pits are going to be larger than anything you or I will be cooking on. Because of the size of their pits, they need to use all hardwood to get the amount of BTUs to sufficiently heat and cook. If you have a large offset smoker, you can cook with all wood. By large smoker, I don't mean a patio model, but rather one that is usually trailer mounted.

Here is the reason we don't recommend using all hardwood to heat your smoker...Most people will build too big a fire in their firebox and the temperature will soar well above where they want to be cooking. So what happens? They begin shutting the firebox dampers to decrease the air flow to the fire. This will decrease the temperature, but it usually starts the wood to smoldering and giving off a dirty smoke because of insufficient combustion. This dirty smoke will ruin even the best piece of meat in only a matter of minutes. The creosote given off by the smoldering fire will settle on the meat's surface. Creosote is what they use to preserve telephone poles. Next time you are outside by a telephone pole, get close and smell the creosote. Do you really want to feed meat with creosote flavor to your family? So let's take a look at what your options are for heating your smoker...

WOOD

The best woods to use as a fuel source are hardwoods. This includes such woods as hickory, oak, and pecan. Hickory, oak, and pecan are also excellent woods for their smoke flavor. Fruitwoods could be used as a fuel source, but their best use would be in combination with either a hardwood or charcoal as the main fuel source. Fruitwoods would include apple, cherry, and peach.

Wood can come in several forms…logs, split logs, wood chunks, chips, and pellets. As a fuel source, wood in the form of logs or split logs is the best choice for providing the most BTUs. Wood chunks can be used to provide heat, but really are better suited for adding smoke flavor. Wood chips provide little heat but a lot of smoke. Wood pellets are a compressed wood product. Some smokers like Cookshack and Traeger use pellets as the heat source and for smoke flavor. There are pellets made by BBQr's Delight that can be used in small grills and smokers, but these are only to add smoke, not heat.

Cooking with all hardwood can be very tricky. The number one mistake most people make while trying to slow cook barbecue is to oversmoke the meat. Remember we want the smoke to flavor and complement the meat flavor. Once meats reach an internal temperature of 160°F, they will not accept any more smoke. Most meats need only a few hours of wood smoke; anything more is asking for trouble.

CHARCOAL BRIQUETTES

Briquettes are made from a mixture of charcoal, ash, and binders such as clay, lime, or starch. Charcoal burns hotter and cleaner than wood. Briquettes also provide a more even heat source than wood or lump charcoal. Charcoal briquettes are also less expensive and more available. We like to use Kingsford charcoal in our smoker. You should never use any charcoal that is an instant light or matchless kind because of the lighter fluid added. With regular charcoal, never use lighter fluid—instead use a charcoal chimney and some newspaper to start your briquettes.

We currently use charcoal briquettes with a combination of wood and wood chunks. Some people will not use charcoal because they say that it gives off a flavor that can be detected in the meat. We've never had that problem. We believe that most people don't give the charcoal enough air flow just as they do with wood. The hotter the fire the cleaner the smoke, we believe.

LUMP CHARCOAL

Lump charcoal is made by heating wood and restricting the fire or oxygen. This process removes water and volatile substances from the wood and leaves the wood looking much like coal. What is left is a material that is almost 90 percent carbon. As with briquettes, the best lump charcoal is made from hardwoods.

Lump charcoal has its advantages over charcoal briquettes. Lump charcoal burns hotter than briquettes and because lump is a more natural product, it burns cleaner than briquettes. Lump charcoal also burns more completely, leaving little ash.

FIRE MANAGEMENT WITH WOOD

Now if you have a large smoker and want to burn all hardwood, here's how you should work your fire. Start by building a fire in your firebox. We cook on a Lang Model 60. This smoker is about five feet long and has a large firebox. The smoker is 1/4" steel throughout and it takes about six logs (about the diameter of a soda can) to get up to temperature (250°F). The logs are stacked to create a box fire. The first two logs are placed on the fire grate with 4 or 5 inches of spacing between them. The next two are spaced the same, but placed perpendicular across the first two logs. The last two are placed on top and they are oriented the same as the first two logs. I usually put chunks of wood or charcoal in the middle to act as dry tinder.

Now to light the fire…to get the fire started will require lots of air flow. So make sure all of your firebox dampers are open, the cooking chamber door is full open, the smokestack damper is full open, and leave the door to the firebox open. We light our fire with a propane weed burner. This can be purchased for less than $30 at your local hardware store (we got ours at Harbor Freight Tools). We set the burner to a medium low setting and use something to prop it so that the flame is shooting right into the center of our box fire. It usually takes five to ten minutes of heat applied to get the wood glowing really hot.

The advantages of using the weed burner is the reduction in the amount of smoke when starting the fire and the length of time it takes to heat up the smoker. If you were to just throw a match on the dry tinder and let the fire build, it would take a long time to heat the smoker and it would create an awful amount of smoke. When you're in a contest setting with people all around, it helps to be a good neighbor by not smoking everyone out when starting the fire. And it is legal to start your pit with gas. Just remember that once the pit is fired and meat placed inside, no gas is allowed at any time thereafter. Note that a few nonsanctioned contests do allow you to cook with gas.

Now once we have the fire burning well and we have removed the gas burner, we can start to close up the smoker. First we wait until the smoke appears white and the cooking area inside the smoker gets up to about 300°F. When this happens we close the cooking chamber door and the firebox door. Because we have decreased the airflow, the smoker temperature will decrease and it will smoke more. We let the smoker build up to about 300° again. By then the smoke will have begun to decrease and we can then put our meat onto the cooker.

We won't cook at 300°, but we overshoot the cooking temperature because once we open the smoker to place the meat, the smoker's temperature will drop drastically.

Now we have our meat on and the temperature is building back up. The firebox dampers are full open and we will gradually close them to get the temperature we desire. If you adjust a damper, allow a few minutes for the temperature to settle. It is best to leave the smokestack damper fully open. Closing the smokestack damper can quickly cause the fire to smolder and give off acrid smoke.

Once we are cooking, it is vital to maintain a consistent temperature in the smoker. Temperature swings too low or high will adversely affect the finished product. We try to not go below 220° or above 250°. We try to cook in the 230° to 240° range. But all cookers react differently and you may have to experiment to find the best temperature for your cooker.

We want to add wood before the temperature begins to drop. We maintain a clean burn by keeping a small flame going in the firebox. Wood that is burning gives off a cleaner smoke than wood that is smoldering. We also split our wood into smaller sticks and lay them on top of the firebox to preheat them before adding to the fire. Smaller sticks that are preheated will catch fire quicker without excessive smoking. Wood prepped this way doesn't waste a lot of thermal energy either. It does mean adding wood more often, but once the smoker reaches temperature it is much easier to maintain. We usually don't have to adjust the smokestack damper once we get going. The vents on the firebox may need to be adjusted occasionally. If you open your vents, more air will be let in creating a hotter fire and the temperature in the cooking area will go up too. Partially closing the vents will lower your temperatures.

FIRE MANAGEMENT WITH CHARCOAL

(lump or briquette)

First let's look at how to start a charcoal fire. Going back to grilling, we all have used a flammable lighter fluid to douse the charcoal prior to lighting. The lighter fluid makes starting the charcoal very easy and we all like to see a big fire! Now as long as you let the coals burn down to white, the lighter fluid is pretty much gone. But why risk tainting your barbecue with lighter fluid aftertaste when there is a better way. And believe me, lighter fluid can flavor your barbecue. I once ate barbecue that an old lady cooked at a roadside shack. The food tasted pretty good, but I could detect an off taste. And then I burped and knew she cooked her meats with charcoal and started with lighter fluid. I asked her how she cooked and sure enough, I was correct.

So here is how you start charcoal without lighter fluid. You use a charcoal chimney. Charcoal chimneys can be purchased anywhere grilling supplies or grills are sold. A chimney holds several pounds of charcoal and is very easy to light. Make sure you read all of the instructions and precautions on the chimney label. One method of lighting is to place a couple of crumpled sheets of newspaper underneath the chimney and light in several places. Some people even go so far as to drizzle a little vegetable oil on the sheets to help it burn longer. It can take fifteen to twenty minutes for the charcoal to become hot coals, but even if you pour them into the smoker before all the coals are hot there is no danger of giving the meat a bad taste from lighter fluid.

With all the dampers fully opened, we pour the hot coals in the firebox. Allow the smoker to heat up to 300°F before adding meats. We overshoot our cooking temperature because opening the smoking chamber to add the meats will lose a lot of heat. Keeping the fire hot will let the pit reheat much more quickly. As the temperature reaches the cooking range desired, we begin to gradually adjust the vents to hold that temperature.

As the fire burns down, we can add more glowing coals to the firebox, but there is an easier way. We can add unburned charcoal directly to the firebox without preburning. This method of adding charcoal can be taken a step further so that we can get long burns without adding coals. This method is referred to as the Minion Method...

First discovered by BBQ expert, Jim Minion, when he was trying to figure out a way to get longer, lower temperature burns on his Weber Smokey Mountain smoker, the Minion Method can be accomplished by placing unlit coals next to lit coals and allowing the hot coals to gradually ignite the unlit coals. Some people will place the unlit coals in their cooker in the shape of a winding snake and place hot coals at one end. It isn't uncommon for smokers to burn for five or six hours using this method.

Cooker manufacturers have even begun to utilize the Minion Method in their design. One of the best examples is the Stump's Smokers. Stump's started building smokers with a charcoal maze—combined with their insulated wall smokers, they could achieve really long charcoal burns. Recently, Stump's has shifted to a gravity feed charcoal system where charcoal is gradually added as it is burned. With their gravity feed systems, Stump's cookers can cook just about anything without ever adding any fuel.

Another company, BBQ Pits by Klose in Texas, builds a charcoal maze box that can be inserted into the firebox of an offset cooker. Their boxes are made from 1/4" steel welded together. We have designed our own charcoal box to fit our smoker. The box is made from plain steel, expanded steel, and stainless steel rivets purchased at Home Depot. We used a bending brake, cordless drill, and a pop rivet tool to assemble the box in a couple of hours. Our firebox isn't 1/4" steel, but it works well enough to get us four- or five-hour burns without adding fuel.

Because we have a large pit, we don't heat up the cooker initially with the charcoal box. Instead we start cooking with all wood. As that initial load of wood begins to burn out, we add a chimney full of hot coals to our "homemade" charcoal box and fill the rest of the box with unlit coals. Before inserting the charcoal box into the smoker, we shovel any hot coals to the back of the firebox and put some into the charcoal box. We have to open the vents all the way until the temperature gets back up and then slowly adjust them to stabilize the temperature.

Because the charcoal doesn't really give that much smoke flavor to the meat, we add chunks of wood into the box. Also as the charcoal in the box burns up, we can add more charcoal to keep the box going longer. Charcoal briquettes create a lot of ash as they burn. This ash can cause such a buildup in the charcoal box that the fire temperature will decrease. We simply stir the box and shake it to make the ash fall to the bottom of the firebox. We then shovel the ash out from under the box so that the fire will get ample air flow.

"FLAVORS" OF WOOD

There are a wide range of woods that can impart flavors from mild and sweet to a very strong, earthy taste. All of the best smoking woods come from hardwood and fruitwood trees. Most people will use what is most common in their area. The Deep South uses mostly hickory and pecan, while Texas uses predominately mesquite. Oak, maple, and cherry are widely available in the North.

Since we use charcoal as our main fuel source, we need to introduce some wood to achieve a smoke flavor. The wood we use is in the form of chunks. These chunks are no larger than a clenched fist. We usually add only a couple of chunks at a time. The wood we use will have an impact on the finished taste of the meat. It is very easy to oversmoke the meat and we believe that less smoke is better. As we cook, the smoke should be light in volume and color. Smoke that is heavy and yellow or dark will cause bad flavors to be imparted. The best smoke is so thin that it appears blue.

You can use just one type of wood for smoke flavor, but we try to use a combination of woods to create a unique taste. We use a mixture of hickory, oak, and apple. The following is a list of the most common smoking woods.

Wood	Flavor	Used for
Mesquite	This is that classic TexMex and Southwestern flavor. It has a strong, biting, zesty flavor.	Use sparingly, as this is the strongest smoking wood. A little goes a long way. I like it on brisket and ribs. Good on chicken too.
Hickory	Hickory is more of a sweet, smoky flavor than mesquite. It is the most popular smoking wood and is what most people would associate with the "classic" American barbecue.	Can be used with any meat especially brisket and pork. Sometimes used in combination with oak for a milder flavor.
Red Oak	Most people describe red oak as a sweeter version of white oak but, overall, oak is not as strong as hickory. Most people would describe oak as a neutral or mellow flavor.	Can be used with any meat and in combination with other woods like hickory and/or fruitwoods. I often think of oak as a heat source rather than a smoke flavor because the other woods are so much more distinct.
White Oak	Similar to red oak, but not quite as sweet a flavor. Can also be found in the form of wine or whiskey barrel chunks. In which case, you would gain the extra aroma of the wine or whiskey.	Same as red oak.
Oak Wine Barrel Blocks (available at www.bbq-book.biz)	A great oaky smoke with a surprisingly strong wine aroma in the smoke.	Great with ribs and chicken but can be used with butts or brisket too.

Pecan	A sweeter, nuttier flavor similar to hickory but not as strong.	Can be used with any meat similar to oak and makes a good stand alone source of heat and flavor.
Maple	A gentle, sweet aroma and flavor.	Great for chicken and pork.
Fruitwoods... apple, cherry, peach, pear, apricot.	These fruitwoods impart a mild, sweet, fruity hint of smoke flavor to your meats.	Usually used with chicken and ribs and can be mixed with oak to add just a touch of the fruity flavor.
Alder	Similar to maple and the fruitwoods. It imparts a subtle, sweet aroma. Some say it has a hint of cedar and that its syrup smells like bananas.	Popular in the Pacific Northwest, it is used a lot to smoke salmon. It can be used for chicken and pork too.
Grapevine	A rich and fruity aroma, as you would expect from a fruitwood.	Mostly used for chicken, wild game, or fish. Popular in the wine regions of the world.
Cedar (planks)	DO NOT burn this in your firebox; rather use it for planking inside your cooking chamber. A sharp, unique, acidic, citrusy flavor.	Mainly used with fish.
Beech	A hardwood similar to oak in flavor.	Use like oak if you have this wood available in your area.
Birch	A softer wood with a flavor similar to maple.	Good for pork and chicken.

Corncob	Usually ground into a powder and used in a foil pack or smoke box. It is strong, so use sparingly as an added flavor combined with other woods. It imparts a sweet flavor.	Good for chicken and fish.
Walnut	Strong, bitter flavor so use sparingly and in combination with other woods.	Used mostly with heavy game.

WOODS NOT SUITABLE FOR SMOKING

As stated before, most hardwood and fruitwood trees are good for smoking. The woods not suitable are needle-bearing trees such as pine and spruce. The smoke from these type trees won't just taste bad, it will make you sick.

Also not a good idea to use for smoking woods are scrap pieces of lumber even if they are hardwoods such as oak, hickory, cherry, or maple. These types of woods can be found in abundance at your local cabinetmaker's shop. They throw tons of this stuff away each year. It is very tempting to use these woods but without knowing if any chemicals were sprayed on them at the lumber mill, you are taking a serious health risk using them for smoking. Best to let sleeping dogs lie.

Wood Bark – Some people feel bark will impart a bitter taste to your meat. I say, you'll probably get a better smoke if you remove it first, so it's safer to remove it "if you can." If it comes off easily, take it off. If it does not come off easily, leave it on. If it is rotten or molded, definitely take it off or do not use that wood.

Age of wood – Your barbecue wood should be between one and six months old. You do not want to use too-green barbecue wood and you also do not want to use barbecue wood that is too dry.

BRINING

Brining causes meat to accept moisture before cooking and helps to retain moisture during cooking. Brine is basically a concentration of salt and sugar within a liquid. Other flavors can be added to the brine, but even a brine with only salt and sugar can dramatically improve a meat's flavor.

There are two basic principles involved in the brining process, osmosis and diffusion. Diffusion and osmosis are always working to reach an equilibrium. Diffusion is what causes the meat to accept the salt and sugar. The concentration of the brine (salt and sugar levels) is greater than the concentration in the meat's tissue. Diffusion tries to reach an equal state of salt and sugar in both the brine and meat. Therefore the salt and sugar levels will increase in the meat's tissue. Brining also causes water to be drawn into the meat. This is because of the higher concentration of water outside the meat trying to equalize with the lower concentration of moisture inside the meat. This movement of moisture is called osmosis.

Once the salt and sugar are in the meat's cells, they cause the proteins to relax and link together. The links of proteins then capture and hold more moisture. As the meat is cooked, the links of proteins begin to gel and form a barrier to lock and hold in moisture and flavor. This is why brined meats taste fresher than nonbrined meats, even after being reheated the next day.

We prefer to use kosher salt and brown sugar in our brines. Kosher salt has a much cleaner taste than table salt and brown sugar gives more flavor than pure sugar. The rule to follow on the ratio of salt to sugar and water is one gallon of water to at least one-half cup of salt (one cup is the maximum) and a minimum of one-half cup of sugar. Brining can cause the meat to be too salty if these proportions are not followed.

The water used in the brine should also be unchlorinated. You can boil tap water for a few minutes to remove most of the chlorine, but it is better to use bottled water. We heat the water to dissolve the salt and sugar. Some of your dry rub can be added also to increase the brine's flavor. Before the meat can be added to the brine, it must be chilled in the refrigerator.

Rule of thumb is about one quart of brine per pound of meat. The best meats to brine are poultry and pork. The meats should be brined for about one hour per pound but no more than eight hours. The best containers to use for brining are large, ziplock freezer bags. Because of contamination by the meat, do not reuse any of the brine.

Rubbery skin on smoked chicken is always a problem to overcome. Brining chicken can add moisture to the skin compounding the problem. Allowing the chicken to air dry in the refrigerator overnight can help evaporate some of the moisture in the skin. This will help the skin cook crisper.

MARINATING AND INJECTING

Marinating is the best way to add flavor to meats. Injecting the marinade into the meat helps to get flavor throughout. Because of the acidic nature of most marinades, it can help tenderize tough cuts of meat. However, using a very acidic marinade for too long can actually cause the meat to be mushy. A marinade will also have oil as an ingredient to help prevent the meat from drying during cooking.

A basic marinade will consist of two to three parts oil to one part acid. Oils commonly used include olive, canola, sunflower, and safflower oil. The acidic part of the marinade can be a vinegar or a citrus fruit juice. The seasonings used in marinades are limited only by your imagination.

On large cuts of meat, marinades will not penetrate very deeply. Injecting marinade into the meat can disperse the flavor throughout. We use a Cajun Injector to inject marinade. It has two large holes in the injection needle to help distribute the marinade more evenly. You may have to strain the marinade prior to injection so that large particles don't clog the needle.

Injecting the marinade is relatively simple. Place the meat on a sheet of plastic wrap. The meat should be face up, just as it would be if placed on the smoker. The meat should be injected at one inch intervals. Insert the needle down into the meat as far as possible without punching through the other side. Then as you slowly pull the injector needle back out of the meat, slowly push down on the plunger. This technique helps to eliminate pockets of marinade in the meat.

After injecting, the meat needs to be placed in the marinade. It is best to use a nonreactive bowl such as plastic. This is because the acid in the marinade will react with a metal container and cause an undesirable flavor. We like to use large, ziplock freezer bags such as a two-gallon size. The bags should be immediately placed in the refrigerator and turned over halfway through marinating. Marinades lose flavor if they are stored for too long, so it is best to make the marinade no more than a day before marinating.

Large cuts of meat can be safely marinated for longer periods than fish or poultry. Beef, chicken, and pork can marinate overnight if the marinade doesn't contain a lot of acid. Usually eight to twelve hours is sufficient. Seafood should be marinated for no more than one hour.

A marinade can also be used as a basting or mop sauce. It is best not to baste with any of the marinade used on the raw meat. It is possible to boil the used marinade to kill any harmful bacteria, but boiling marinade can cause it to lose flavor intensity. It is best to make extra marinade to be used as a basting sauce.

Here's a sample recipe:

Pork Marinade and Inject:

2 cups apple juice
2/3 cup Worcestershire sauce
1 tbsp Texas Pete Hot Sauce
2 tbsp Moore's Marinade

Many other liquids can be used, including...red wine vinegar, soy sauce, vinegar, sherry, wine, beer, Italian salad dressing, lemon or lime juice, Worcestershire sauce, catsup, honey, molasses, cane syrup, maple syrup, whiskey, Tabasco, apple cider vinegar, apple cider or juice, olive oil, pineapple juice, hoisin sauce, sesame oil, orange juice, balsamic vinegar, grape juice, etc. You can use fresh vegetables and fruits like onion, garlic, ginger, raspberry, blackberry, etc. And don't forget about all of your spices like sugar, salt, pepper, and many more like those listed in the "rubs" section below...

RUBS

Many teams spend a lot of time and money to create their own rubs. Early on we decided to spend more time honing our cooking techniques and less time trying to create a unique rub. We've tried a lot of different brand rubs that were really outstanding. We tried to find one that fit the flavor we were trying to create in our barbecue.

One common mistake is to think that one rub can be used for all four meat categories. The salt and sugar levels as well as the spices need to be changed for chicken, pork, ribs, and brisket. We use Cookshack Spicy Chicken Rub, Cookshack Spicy BBQ Sauce Mix on pork as a dry rub, HomeBBQ Rib Rub, and HomeBBQ Beef Rub on brisket.

A rub can be thought of as a dry marinade. The purpose of marinating is to infuse flavor into the meat. A dry rub does the same thing...add flavor. The applied rub draws moisture out of the meat and the two combine on the surface of the meat and form a wet paste. If the meat is wrapped in plastic wrap and refrigerated, the paste on the surface is pulled back down into the meat. The paste on the surface will also form a crust on the meat as it is cooked. This crust, also called bark, is valued by BBQ cooks for its flavor.

So let's look at how we apply the rubs. The best way to apply dry rub is by using a shaker container like the ones pizza places use for Parmesan cheese. First we lay a piece of wax paper down on a table and then a piece of plastic wrap on top of the wax paper. To help the rub stick on the meat, we apply a binder all over the meat. A binder is a wet substance that causes the rub to stay on the meat. We use an aerosol cooking spray as a binder. Some teams use yellow mustard, olive oil, vegetable oil, and even Worcestershire sauce. With the meat on the plastic wrap, we shake the rub onto it. We don't want to rub the seasoning into the meat because this clogs the pores of the meat and keeps the smoke and flavors from being pulled down into the meat. As we wrap the meat in the plastic wrap, any loose rub is put back on the meat.

Rubs can be applied for longer periods of time on large cuts such as pork butts and brisket. Some people apply rubs more than twenty-four hours before they cook. In competition we don't have that much time for the rub to sit on the meat before we have to start cooking. We don't apply the rub on ribs until about an hour before we start to cook them. If rub is applied for too long on ribs, there is a danger that the salt in the rub could cause the ribs to dry out when cooking.

We also apply the rub on chicken just before cooking because we have them marinating until we are ready to cook.

Here's a sample basic rub recipe...

Basic Rub:

16 tsp brown sugar
3 tsp kosher salt
1 tsp chili powder
3 tsp sweet paprika
½ tsp granulated garlic
½ tsp onion powder
¼ tsp cayenne pepper
¼ tsp black pepper

Rib Rub:

1 cup granulated brown sugar
2 tsp white sugar
¼ tsp cayenne pepper
1 tbsp chili powder
1 tsp black pepper
2 tsp granulated garlic
1 tsp granulated onion
½ tsp nutmeg
½ tsp cinnamon
1 tsp Country Time Lemonade mix

Beef Rub:

1 cup of granulated garlic
⅓ cup of black pepper
¼ cup of kosher salt
⅓ cup of chili powder
2 tbsp of chipotle pepper

Note on beef rub: This rub is for cooking brisket hot and fast so it has no sugars. If you want to cook at lower temps, you can add ½ cup of turbinado sugar.

Chicken Rub:

4 tbsp granulated brown sugar
2 tsp kosher salt
1 tbsp granulated garlic
1 tbsp black pepper
1 tbsp sweet Hungarian paprika
2 tbsp Old Bay Seasoning
1 tsp ancho chili powder

Pork Rub:

3 cups of turbinado sugar
½ cup plus 2 tbsp of kosher salt
4 tbsp of sweet Hungarian paprika
1 tbsp of black pepper
1 tbsp of chili powder
1 tsp of chipotle pepper
1 tbsp of cayenne pepper
1 tbsp of granulated onion
2 tsp of granulated garlic
1 tsp of oregano

Memphis-style rib rub:

5 tsp. sweet Hungarian paprika
2 tsp kosher salt
1 tsp black pepper
1 tsp cayenne pepper
1 tsp chili powder
1 tsp garlic granules
1 tsp onion powder
(Makes about ¼ cup of rub)

Kansas City-style rib rub:

¼ cup brown sugar or turbinado sugar
1 tbsp kosher salt
1 tbsp sweet Hungarian paprika

1 tsp chili powder
½ tsp garlic granules
½ tsp onion powder
¼ tsp black pepper
¼ tsp red pepper
(Makes about ½ cup of rub)

As you can imagine with all the ingredients and spices available, there are literally millions of different combinations or recipes you can make. Don't be afraid to experiment with what you like. And don't forget about the binder or "glue"—you can use mustard, honey, melted butter, olive oil, or any combination that you think would work well. If you like things hot, add in a little bit more cayenne, jalapeno, chipotle, or even dried habanero. Other ingredients include fennel, coriander, cinnamon, turmeric, sage, dill, rosemary, parsley, basil, oregano, cumin, celery salt, Mrs. Dash, red pepper flakes, lemon pepper, allspice, cloves, star anise, thyme, dry mustard, ancho, nutmeg, Cajun spice (file´—*fee-lay*—powder), etc.

FINISHING SAUCES

We use a finishing sauce on our ribs and chicken in competitions. These meats benefit greatly from sauce cooked onto their surface, whereas pork butts and brisket don't benefit as much. The sauces we use could best be described as glazes. Appearance of the meat is not only important for judging purposes; it improves the taste too...The first thing we as humans do is judge how well something may taste by how it looks. If it looks good it may taste good, but if it looks bad we quickly assume it tastes bad.

Our chicken sauce is actually easy to make. We use one cup of Ken's Raspberry Walnut Vinaigrette Salad Dressing, one cup of ketchup, and one cup of honey. Mix these all together. You can store in the refrigerator, but the honey tends to settle to the bottom. It's better to make the sauce right before using. We apply the sauce several times during the last hour of cooking. The honey gives the chicken a very nice sheen and the salad dressing gives a unique flavor. The ketchup helps to make the sauce taste more like a barbecue sauce and not just a salad dressing.

On ribs, we combine one-quarter cup of honey with one cup of Ole Ray's Apple/Cinnamon BBQ Sauce. As with the chicken, the honey gives a nice glaze on the ribs. We also apply the sauce several times during the last hour of cooking. Allowing the sauce to cook onto the ribs contributes to a better finished product than just brushing on some sauce after the ribs have finished cooking. For one, the sugars in the sauce begin to caramelize...adding to the flavor. Also...the color of the sauce darkens, which increases the visual impact of the ribs.

REGIONAL BARBECUE SAUCE VARIATIONS

In the US, there are distinct BBQ sauce regions, each with its own flavor variations of BBQ sauces. Sometimes, when traveling to competitions, it may help to know what type of barbecue the local judges like. Most BBQ contest judges are from the local area, so if you are near Kansas City, where they like a sweet sauce and/or rub, don't give them a Texas spicy sauce or rub. This distinct BBQ geography breaks down something like this...

- Kansas City – Along with Memphis, this is probably one of the two most popular BBQ regions. In Kansas City, they are known for their sweet and spicy tomato-based BBQ sauce, usually containing molasses.

  Kansas City-Style BBQ Sauce:

  3 cups ketchup
  ½ cup dark brown sugar
  ½ cup water
  ½ cup white wine vinegar
  ½ cup tomato paste
  2 tbsp yellow mustard
  2 tbsp chili powder
  1 tbsp freshly ground pepper
  1 tsp salt
  1 tsp granulated onion powder
  1 tsp granulated garlic powder
  ½ tsp ground ginger
  ½ tsp cayenne

  Mix all ingredients together and simmer for 30 minutes. Makes about 4 cups.

- Memphis – Maybe the most popular BBQ region, but I bet the Kansas City folks would disagree. But certainly, everyone would agree that Memphis and Kansas City are #1 and #2 (but who knows what order). Memphis is probably known more for their dry rubbed ribs, but they do have their own distinct BBQ sauce flavor too. It's not quite as sweet as a Kansas City BBQ sauce, but it is vinegar and tomato based. It's usually a thinner sauce with a little brown sugar and mustard thrown in for taste.

Memphis-Style BBQ Sauce:

3 tbsp butter
2 tsp onion powder
2 - 15-oz cans tomato sauce
1 cup cider vinegar
⅓ cup Worcestershire sauce
½ cup lemon juice
½ tsp Tabasco
½ cup brown sugar
1 tsp mustard powder
1 tbsp black pepper
1 tbsp chili powder
1 tsp salt
½ tsp cayenne

Mix all ingredients and simmer for 30 minutes. Makes 4 cups sauce.

- Texas – Now you're getting into beef territory. Brisket is king here. Texas is a big state and, generally, you'll find a more spicy BBQ sauce there. In East Texas, you might find more sweet sauces with a little bit of chili. Mainly ketchup based with Worcestershire. On the west side of Texas, you run into hotter chili-based sauces with a tomato base.

Texas-Style Barbecue Sauce:

¼ lb butter or margarine
1 cup vinegar
1 cup water
½ cup tomato ketchup
2 tsp Worcestershire sauce
1 tsp dry mustard
2 tsp chili powder
¼ tsp cayenne
1 tsp black pepper
1 tsp salt
¼ cup sugar
2 crushed bay leaves
2 cloves garlic, minced

1 large onion, grated
Juice of 1 lemon

Mix all ingredients and simmer for 15 minutes. Makes about 2 cups.

- Western North Carolina and Virginia – There isn't much difference between western North Carolina BBQ sauce and eastern North Carolina BBQ sauce. In the west, they add a little tomato base to the sauce. Other than that, it's mostly vinegar with some salt, red pepper flakes, or cayenne pepper added to taste.

- Upper South Carolina and Eastern North Carolina – As stated above, this is usually a thin vinegar-based sauce with salt, red pepper, or cayenne pepper added to taste.

Carolina Vinegar BBQ Sauce:

1 cup distilled white vinegar
1 cup cider vinegar
1 tbsp sugar
1 tbsp crushed red pepper flakes
1 tbsp hot red pepper flakes
Salt and ground pepper to taste

Mix all ingredients, including salt and pepper, to taste, in medium bowl. Makes 2 cups.

- Lower South Carolina - Home of the yellow mustard and vinegar-based BBQ sauce. Sometimes a little ketchup is thrown in too but it is primarily a mustard-based sauce.

Mustard BBQ Sauce:

4 cups yellow mustard
8 ounces of beer
½ cup apple cider vinegar
8 tbsp brown sugar
½ cup tomato puree
2 tsp Worcestershire sauce
1 tbsp cayenne
1 tbsp fresh cracked black pepper
2 tsp salt

1½ tsp garlic powder
Heat all ingredients in a saucepan over medium heat and mix well. Makes 6 cups.

- Georgia – Some people say that Georgia is sort of a melting pot of BBQ sauces. Being situated between Tennessee, South Carolina, Alabama, and Florida, we sort of like all kinds of BBQ sauce down here. Heck...we even like a Texas hot and spicy sauce every now and then. If I had to pick one BBQ sauce that would best describe a "Georgia BBQ sauce," I guess it would be a ketchup, mustard, vinegar-based sauce.

My Mom's Barbecue Sauce:

One small to medium onion, chopped
1½ cups ketchup
1½ cup water
¼ cup vinegar
½ tsp salt
1 tsp paprika
½ tsp black pepper
1 tsp chili powder
¼ cup Worcestershire sauce
1 tsp yellow mustard

Combine everything in a large saucepan, mixing well. Bring to a boil and then simmer, uncovered, several hours until thick. Makes about 2 cups.

- Florida – In the Citrus State, you know they are going to throw in a little lemon and lime. So...Florida is a tomato-based sauce, on the sour side, with notes of lemon and/or lime.

Florida Citrus BBQ Sauce:

1 tbsp olive oil
½ cup diced onion
2 tsp minced garlic
1 pinch ground cloves
1 pinch ground cinnamon
1 tbsp chili powder
1 cup orange juice

1 cup ketchup
2 tbsp molasses
1 tbsp Worcestershire sauce
¼ tsp cayenne pepper

Heat olive oil in medium-sized saucepan. Add onion and garlic and sauté until onions are translucent. Add cloves, cinnamon, chili powder and orange juice to saucepan and bring to a boil. Add remaining ingredients and simmer until sauce thickens, 5-10 minutes. Makes about 2 cups.

- Alabama – They like a spicy tomato-based BBQ sauce in Alabama. And, of course, Alabama is the one and only state to claim the famous white mayonnaise-based BBQ sauce.

White BBQ Sauce:

1 cup mayonnaise
1 cup cider vinegar
1 tbsp lemon juice
1½ tbsp black pepper
½ tsp salt
¼ tsp cayenne

Mix ingredients together and refrigerate for at least 8 hours before using. Makes about 2 cups.

- Kentucky – A unique BBQ sauce used often in Kentucky is a black Worcestershire and vinegar-based sauce. Also popular are tomato-based sauces with a touch of bourbon added just for flavor.

Bourbon BBQ Sauce:

¼ cup Wild Turkey Bourbon
2 cups ketchup
1 cup brown sugar
½ cup apple cider vinegar
¼ cup pineapple juice
3 tsp molasses
2 tsp Worcestershire sauce
2 tsp olive oil
1 tsp lemon juice
1 tsp salt

Mix all ingredients and simmer on stove until sauce thickens. Makes about 4 cups.

- Southwest – Salsa-like tomato-based sauces are popular with a Mexican influence. Southwest BBQ sauces have a little "kick" to them.

Spicy Southwest BBQ Sauce:

6 cloves garlic
2 cups ketchup
2 stalks celery
1 cup water
½ cup onion, chopped
½ cup brown sugar
½ cup butter or margarine
½ cup Worcestershire sauce
½ cup cider vinegar
3 tbsp chili powder
2 tsp instant coffee granules
2 tsp dried crushed red pepper
½ tsp salt
½ tsp ground cloves

Bake garlic in a small baking pan at 350°F for 20 to 30 minutes or until lightly browned. Cool and peel. Combine garlic and remaining ingredients in a saucepan. Simmer for 20 minutes. Cool. Process mixture in a blender until smooth. Makes about 4 cups.

- Louisiana – They like it hot and spicy down there. A spiced-up version of a thick tomato-based sauce is popular with Cajun and Creole flavors.

Cajun BBQ Sauce:

1 tsp black pepper
1 tsp kosher salt
1 tsp onion powder
1 tsp garlic powder
½ tsp white pepper
½ tsp cayenne
½ lb sliced bacon
1 cup onion

2 cups beef stock
1 cup chili sauce
1 cup honey
5 tsp fresh orange juice
1 tsp orange zest
2 tsp fresh lemon juice
1 tsp lemon zest
2 tsp garlic puree
¼ cup unsalted butter

Cook bacon until crisp. Sauté onions until caramelized. Add remaining ingredients. Heat and stir for 20-25 minutes. Cool. Process in a food processor or blender until smooth. Makes about 5 cups.

- Hawaiian – Sweet and sour in a tomato base, of course. Pineapple is popular along with other tropical fruits.

Hawaiian BBQ Sauce:

⅓ cup unsweetened pineapple juice
¼ cup teriyaki sauce
¼ cup ketchup
1 garlic clove, minced
1 tbsp brown sugar
1 tbsp ginger, minced

Combine all ingredients in a saucepan and simmer for 15 minutes. Makes about 1 cup.

CHICKEN

Smoked chicken cooks quicker and is probably the cheapest meat to smoke. Therefore we will begin our BBQ lessons on chicken. Chicken can be smoked as a whole chicken, halves, quarters, or as individual pieces. Chicken is a pretty blank canvas that allows for wide range of style and flavor. We will discuss how to get flavor not just on the surface of the meat, but how to get flavors and moisture deep down into the meat.

HOW TO BUY

The majority of the chickens raised in US today are either from the Cornish (an English breed) or White Rock breed (developed in New England). Chicken falls into categories based on age, weight, and sex.

- Broiler / Fryer – chickens that are around seven weeks old with a weight from 2.5 to 4.5 lb. These are very young and tender chickens that can be cooked by almost any method.

- Rock Cornish Game Hen – small broiler/fryers that weigh 1 to 2 lb.

- Roaster – chickens that are three to five months old weighing 5 to 7 lb. Good for roasting whole.

- Capon – males that are four to eight months old. Weights vary from 4 to 7 lb. Meat is light and tender and is usually roasted.

- Stewing or baking hen – ten- to eighteen-month-old laying hens. Best used for stewing due to meat not being as tender as young hens.

- Cock or rooster – mature male chickens. Meat is dark and tough. Skin is coarse. Needs to be cooked for long period of time with moist environment.

ALL NATURAL, FREE RANGE, AND ORGANIC.

- "All natural" is a description found on packaged chicken. The term means that the fresh chicken has been cleaned and readied to cook with as little handling as possible. The chickens are also fed a USDA-approved feed formula of natural ingredients that meet exacting standards.

- "Free-range" chickens are allowed access outside the chicken house. With their food and water inside the chicken house, they usually don't wander far.

- USDA has strict standards for "organic" labeled chicken. From the second day of an organic chicken's life, it cannot be medicated (vaccination is allowed, however) and must be fed only organic ingredients. Organic chickens must also be given access to the outdoors (free range).

FRESH OR FROZEN

Chicken that has never been below 26°F can be labeled as fresh. Chicken that has been taken to 0°F or below must be labeled as frozen or previously frozen. Ironically poultry stored between 0°F and 25°F requires no specific labeling.

PACKAGED CHICKEN

All chicken sold retail has been inspected by government agencies for signs of disease. Chicken should have a seal that reads "Inspected for wholesomeness by the USDA." This inspection is mandatory by the government, but grading of chicken is not mandated by the government. Grading is a voluntary procedure. USDA Grade A chickens have been graded based on meeting the USDA Marketing Services criteria. Grade A chickens have plump, meaty bodies and clean skin, free of bruises, broken bones, feathers, cuts and discoloration.

Speaking of skin color, what is the correct skin color of wholesome chicken, cream color or yellow? The answer is both and all shades of color in between. The color of a chicken's skin is based on what the chicken is fed. The skin color is not a reflection of the wholesomeness, flavor, tenderness, or fat content. Some parts of the country will favor a certain skin color for their chicken purchases. The growers will try to feed their chickens a diet that will produce the most pleasing skin color to the purchasers of their chickens.

Another misconception is that pink liquid in packaged chicken is blood. A chicken that wasn't bled properly would have cherry red skin and it would be condemned at the processing plant. A properly bled chicken will have very small amount of blood left in muscle tissue. The pink liquid is mostly water that has been absorbed during the chilling process mixed with this very small amount of blood. An excessive amount of liquid could be a sign that the meat has been frozen and thawed.

COOKING CHICKEN

This is how we cook chicken step by step...First, we cook only chicken thighs. White meat tends to dry out much quicker than dark meat. Also dark meat tends to accept the flavors well that we try to introduce to them through marinating.

We begin by washing and trimming the thighs. As we lay the thighs skin side down on a cutting board, we look for any large pads of fat or anything that doesn't look pleasing to the eye and we cut these imperfections away. We try to select thighs that are mostly the same size so that they will all cook in the same amount of time. Sometimes a little bit of the meat on either side of the bone may have to be trimmed to keep a uniform size. Now we turn the thighs over so that the skin is up. Because the skin will shrink as it cooks, we want to use our palms to press out the skin all around the thighs. This will help to stretch the skin out. We want enough skin to completely cover the thighs on top and all sides. Trim away any excess skin.

Next we marinate the chicken in a salad dressing. Chicken is a pretty blank canvas and readily accepts a wide range of flavors. Wishbone Italian dressing is a good choice. The bottle of dressing should be chilled to below 40°F before being placed on the chicken. We use one-gallon freezer bags to hold the chicken and marinade. While marinating, the chicken should be kept below 40°F to avoid bacteria growing. The chicken is marinated for three or four hours and the marinade is discarded afterward.

After marinating, don't rinse the marinade off the chicken—just pat off the excess. The marinade left on the chicken will become a binder for the next step, which is to sprinkle a rub on the chicken. You can develop your own rub, but there are many good commercially available rubs to choose from. We like to use Cookshack Spicy Chicken Rub. We sprinkle the rub on the back and skin side of the chicken and then we lift the skin and get some of the rub between the skin and meat. You may have to use your fingers to help push the rub under the skin.

Now the chicken is ready to be smoked. We normally smoke most meats at 225°–250°F, but chicken cooks better at a 275°-300° range. Chicken accepts smoke very easily. Most people overdo the smoke. Cooking at a higher temperature helps to avoid this and also helps with the other smoked chicken problem— rubbery skin. One solution to rubbery skin is to place the chicken over a hot grill for a very short time after smoking. What we try to do is raise the smoker temperature and cook the chicken enough to render the fat under the skin. The skin will still not be crispy like a grilled chicken, but it will be more like a rotisserie chicken.

We must also choose our smoking wood. We prefer to use a mixture of hickory and apple in a ratio of 25 to 75 percent, respectively. Apple wood just gives a much sweeter smoke flavor, but it is very mild. A little hickory seems to boost the smoke flavor. We try to introduce the smoke during the first one and a half hours of cooking—after that we don't add any more wood for smoke (just charcoal or whatever you are using for heat).

We start the chicken skin side up. As we place each thigh on the smoker, we try to roll the skin around the thighs tucking the extra skin on the sides up underneath. This will help to create an envelope to seal in the juices. After cooking the chicken for one hour, we open the smoker and spray the thighs with apple juice. The caramelizing of the sugars in the apple juice will help to develop a nice golden brown skin. We also turn the thighs over after the first hour. We spray the chicken with apple juice again in another thirty minutes. After two hours' cooking time, we glaze the bottom of the thighs and turn over and glaze the skin side. The glaze we use is a very simple one that gives a unique flavor. We combine equal parts honey, ketchup, and a raspberry vinaigrette salad dressing. We will glaze the skin side of the chicken once more in fifteen minutes and then continue to cook for another fifteen to forty-five minutes to achieve doneness.

Correctly done, the characteristics of the chicken will be that the meat will be very tender and moist, the meat should separate cleanly off the bone and the bone should turn white, the skin should be edible in bites, and all the flavors we have introduced to the chicken should combine into one pleasing flavor.

Finished chicken in competition that allows garnishments...

PORK RIBS

There are two categories of pork ribs...The loin back ribs that come from the area closest to the backbone of the pig and the spareribs that come from the lower part of the rib cage. True baby back ribs are loin back ribs that weigh 1.75 lb. or less. Today most loin back ribs are called baby backs even though they weigh more. We cook spareribs only because we feel they have more marbling of fat that gives them more flavor and moisture. Because of the extra fat, spareribs are more forgiving when overcooked. It doesn't hurt that they are a lot less expensive either!

Spareribs contain the rib bones with the brisket attached (which is part of the sternum) and a flap of meat, called the skirt, connected on the bone side of the slab. Loin back ribs don't have any attachments to the slab. They are much easier to prepare to cook. Just remove the membrane on the bone side and trim any excess fat. We cook only spareribs and will go into more details on prepping them. All of our methods of prep and cooking also apply to loin back ribs with the exception of removing brisket and flap.

For presentation purposes we cut our spareribs to resemble loin back ribs. This cut is called the St. Louis-style cut. This cut also creates a more uniform rack of ribs that look nicer and cook more evenly (see the chapter on trimming spareribs for detailed pictures). To make this cut, place the slab bone side up. Starting at the sternum end (the larger rib bones are at this end), cut between the bone and cartilage at the joint. Follow the joints down the slab to create a uniform width slab. After removing the brisket, we trim away the skirt meat. Some people call this slab, minus brisket and skirt, a Kansas City-style slab, but we won't squabble over terminology.

Now we need to remove the membrane on the bone side of the slab. Starting again at the sternum end, use a butter knife to pry up the membrane. You will notice a second membrane underneath, but do not remove this membrane. Removing the top membrane will make the ribs more tender. It also allows for more flavors and smoke to penetrate. The second membrane is not very tough, but it does help hold the meat and bones together during cooking. Once you get the top membrane pried up, grab it with a dry paper towel and slowly pull across the slab to remove it. If you are lucky it will all come off in one piece. If not, just remove all of the membrane pieces. One tip is to make sure your ribs are very cold when removing the membrane. It seems to come off easier on very cold slabs.

Before turning the ribs over, we scrape away any excessive areas of fat. Now turn the slab meat side up and we need to address the fat on this side. Most of the excessive fat will be at the sternum end over the first two ribs. At this end there will usually be a layer of meat with a heavy fat pad below. We trim off this small strip of meat and most of the fat. Trimming this area also makes the slab a more uniform thickness that helps in even cooking. Now is the time to make sure any ragged areas are trimmed up and check for any blood vessels usually at the end of the slab. Any of these can be trimmed off the slab.

At this point the ribs could go on the smoker, but we want to add flavor. We do this by applying a dry rub seasoning. Before we apply the rub, we need a binder to keep the rub on the ribs. Examples of binders are yellow mustard (just like what you put on hot dogs), Worcestershire sauce, soy sauce, and what we prefer to use, cooking spray such as PAM. Lightly spray the ribs all over, both sides, ends, and edges.

We have made many good rubs, but we prefer to use a commercially available rib rub. There are so many rubs out there to choose from that are really good. So you'll just have to experiment to find one that fits your taste. We prefer to use a rub that is not overly spicy. After spraying with the oil, we lightly sprinkle the rub on all surfaces of the ribs. A rub that doesn't contain a high salt content can be left on the ribs overnight before smoking by wrapping the slab in plastic wrap and refrigerating. If the rub is high in salt, leaving it on too long before smoking can cause the meat to dry out and be tough. It may even make the ribs taste hammy. We try to apply our rib rub just after starting the smoker up. The smoker takes about an hour to fully heat up and this gives us time to get the rub on and allow the ribs to warm up before smoking.

We aim for a temperature of 230° to 240° for our ribs. Sometimes the temperature may drop to 220° or shoot up to 250° for a few minutes, but we can quickly stabilize the temperature without harming the ribs. The real key to creating good barbecue is to keep the temperatures as even as possible. For smoke flavor we use a mixture of hickory (25 percent), oak (25 percent), and apple (50 percent). We apply smoke only during the first three hours of cooking. After that we don't apply anymore smoking woods.

We start the ribs cooking by placing them meat side up to start. We cook them for two hours before spraying them with apple juice and turning them over and spraying the bone side. Waiting two hours before spraying ribs allows the rub to set and not be washed off by the spray.

After three hours' total cook time, we remove the ribs and place them bone side up on a sheet of heavy aluminum foil. We generously spray the ribs down with apple juice and tightly wrap them up in the foil. The foiled ribs are placed back on the smoker bone side up. The slabs are cooked for another hour before checking for tenderness. We check for tenderness by inserting a toothpick in the ribs. Knowing when the ribs are tender enough is very subjective, but you'll gain the knowledge with experience. One thing you might want to look for is the meat pulling away from the bone—this is a sure sign that your ribs are getting done. Maybe gently tug on one of the bones to see if it is "loose." Also...if you pick up one end of a slab with a pair of tongs and your slab bends down 90°, then that is another sign that your ribs are getting done.

Most of the time, one hour in foil will render the ribs tender, but at times you may have to go one and a quarter to one and a half hours. What you don't want to do is cook the ribs so long in the foil that the meat falls away from the bones. If you try to lift the ribs out of the foil and they fall apart then they either went too long in the foil or your temperature was too high.

At this point the ribs have cooked for four to four and a half hours and are very tender. The next step will be to "finish" them with a glaze sauce. At this stage you don't want your fire to be too hot. It is better to err on the low side to keep from burning the BBQ sauce glaze. We remove the ribs from the foil and place them back on the smoker. We use a sauce mop to apply the glaze on both sides of the meat. Any favorite BBQ sauce can be used for the glaze. We prefer a sauce that has an apple/cinnamon flavor to complement our rub and smoke flavors as well as the apple juice used earlier. To create a glaze just add one-quarter cup of honey to a cup of your favorite BBQ sauce. The honey will create a nice sheen on the ribs as the sugars caramelize and will add to the overall flavor. We apply the glaze again in thirty minutes and allow it to fully set for the last thirty minutes of cooking. So...to recap cooking times, we cook three hours before wrapping ribs in foil and cooking one to one and a half hours in foil. We then remove from foil and glaze ribs for the last hour.

Finished ribs in competition that allows garnishments...

Finished ribs (no garnishment) – note the technique used in cutting the ribs: you can either cut three ribs and just remove the outer two bones and trim evenly for appearance or just cut one bone out cutting as close as possible to the two adjacent bones so you don't turn in any bones that don't have any meat on them...

PORK BUTTS AND SHOULDERS

We use bone-in Boston butt roasts for competitions. Some teams cook whole shoulders; however, butts cook much quicker and we believe the best parts of the shoulder come mainly from the butt roast. There are competitions that require you to cook the whole shoulder such as Memphis in May. We have cooked shoulders and our technique is basically the same as how we do butts.

In selecting butts, we try to choose butts in the seven- to nine-pound weight range. We look for pork that has a nice pink color while avoiding the butts with a deeper red color. The butt should have an even layer of fat on one side and noticeable fat marbling in the meat. We try to make sure not to select butts where the bone is broken or crumbling into fragments on the end. You don't want to serve pork with bits of bone mixed in with the meat. Also look the meat over for any large blood clots. We try to avoid a butt if there appears to be any blood showing on the outside of the meat.

We also use fresh, never frozen, pork butts because we believe they cook up more tender and moist than frozen ones. It is very hard to find these in supermarkets. That is why we purchase almost all of our meats from meat markets that know the meats haven't been frozen. These guys are real butchers and the guys in most supermarkets are not really that knowledgeable about meats since most of their meats come prepackaged.

One last thing we look for in pork is the lack of enhancements and added solutions to the meat. Supposedly these were added to increase shelf life and preserve flavor. Two problems with these solutions...First is you're paying for water by the pound. Add in the bone and all the fat that you can't eat and the meat gets pricey really quick. Second, the solutions usually contain salt and preservatives that cause the pork butt to taste too much like ham when cooked.

Trimming and prepping butts is fairly easy. The most important things to look for on pork are any glands or lymph nodes. These are usually on the sides of the butt and are easily cut away. Just be careful not to cut or burst them because they can leave a bitter or bad taste in the meat. We also cut away any blood vessels that are visible on the butts and wash away any visible signs of blood.

Some teams will remove the fat cap on butts. Their thinking is that the internal fat of the butts is sufficient to keep the meat moist. It is true that the internal fat will render and help to keep the meat moist, but we like the added benefits of leaving the fat cap on. As the fat cap renders, the juices flow down and around the meat, which creates a self baste. Leaving the fat cap on can help to insulate the meat from excessive heat and smoke. Some of the best-tasting meat are the small strips dispersed in the fat cap.

After the butt has been trimmed, we move on to injecting the butt. In a competition, time is limited. Ideally we would like to brine the butts overnight to get moisture and flavor deep down into the meat. One way to overcome this time limitation is to manually put the brine or flavoring deep into the pork.

We do this with a marinade or meat injector. You can spend a couple of dollars on a cheap injector, but you'll be lucky to get a couple of uses before it falls apart. Commercial meat injectors can cost more than $100. We've tried them all until we found this little injector. Actually we saw several pro teams using these injectors on one of the BBQ television shows and decided to try one. It's called a Cajun Injector.

We inject our pork with a blend of one cup apple juice, one-half cup soy sauce, and one-half cup Worcestershire sauce. The injection solution needs to be cold before injection to avoid raising the temperature into the danger zone too long. The danger zone is between 40° and 140°F. Meat in this temperature range should be either heated above or cooled below as soon as possible.

It takes about two cups of injection solution per butt. We insert the injector into the fat side of the butt at about one-inch intervals. The injector needle is plunged as deeply as possible without punching through the other side. The needle is then slowly pulled back up while lightly depressing the injector plunger. Injecting this way will keep the solution from puddling in one spot.

As stated previously, we cook the butts fat cap up during the entire smoke. By keeping our inject holes on the top there is less chance of the solution cooking out of the butts. The injection holes also allow the fat cap to render and flow down into the butts. All of this helps to keep our pork butts very moist and flavorful.

After injecting the pork, we wrap it in plastic wrap and store in an ice chest until about an hour before placing on the smoker. Once we are ready to smoke the butt, we remove it from the cooler and plastic wrap and apply a dry rub all over the butt. The rub we use is Cookshack Spicy Barbecue Sauce Mix (we use it as a dry rub). Most pork rubs use heavy paprika and red peppers as their base.

The rub we use doesn't have a heavy red/orange color, but rather a light brown color. It complements pork better than any rub we have used.

We are now ready to cook the pork. The smoker is kept at 230° to 240° and we try to place the butts as far away from the firebox as possible. This helps to keep the butts from cooking too quickly and drying out. And remember they are cooked fat cap up. The butts cook for three or four hours before we spray them with apple juice. It's best if the apple juice is heated before spraying it on the butts.

Even though we spray the butts during the cooking process, it isn't critical to do so because of the amount of fat on the butts. We just think it adds to the flavor and we spray the butts only when we have the smoker open. We never open the smoker just to spray any meats. As the saying goes, "*If you're lookin', you ain't cookin'.*" Opening the smoker allows valuable heat to escape and only adds to the overall cooking time.

Some people put their pork butts on and do nothing to them until they are done. Pork butts require only low and steady heat for a long period of time. The smoker does the magic of rendering the fat, breaking down the collagen in the meat muscles, and giving pork its wonderful flavor and tenderness. It's really hard to mess up a butt. Even if we overcook it the flavor is always great.

Pork butts generally take eight to twelve hours or one to one and a half hours per pound. We cook our pork until it reaches an internal temperature of 195°. There are two tests that can check for doneness and tenderness...One is if the blade bone feels loose in the meat and the other is if the pork wiggles like Jell-O when pressed on. You know the pork is perfect when the blade bone slides out of the meat easily without any meat attached.

Once the meat is done, we apply a sauce to the butts. We use a cup of Big Bob Gibson's Red Sauce and add a quarter cup of honey. The sauce is lightly applied to the butts and then we wrap them in plastic wrap to hold in the moisture. The butts are then wrapped with aluminum foil and placed in a cooler to hold the temperature until time to pull the pork. Meat can be safely held for hours in a cooler, but we recommend inserting an electronic temperature probe so that the meat temperature can be monitored without opening the cooler. For safety reasons, the meat should be held at 140° or above.

When we are ready to pull the pork, we take the butts out of the cooler and remove the aluminum foil. Leaving the plastic wrap helps retain moisture as

the butts cool and the juices flow back into the meat. In competitions, we try to pull the pork into large chunks. We want eight large hunks of meat for the judges to choose from. We also shred some of the pork to place in the presentation box.

If we were cooking to cater or at home, we would just shred all of the pork in a pan and drizzle some of the Big Bob Gibson Red Sauce (no honey is added) over the top of the meat and toss to coat evenly. When done properly, the meat doesn't look as if sauce has been added.

Pork freezes and reheats very well, but first the meat must be shredded or chopped. We like to add the sauce before placing the meat in one-gallon freezer bags. It helps to try to push as much air out of the freezer bag as possible. To reheat, remove bag from freezer and place in the refrigerator to thaw. The pork can be warmed by placing the whole bag in a pot of water on a medium low heat.

BEEF BRISKET

HOW TO BUY

A whole brisket consists of two parts, the flat and the point, also called the deckle. Whole briskets will have one side that is covered in a heavy fat pad. Brisket flats can be purchased minus the point and it may or may not have one side covered in fat.

Beef is primarily divided into three grades. These grades are Select, Choice, and Prime. Not sure if there is such a thing as Prime brisket. Not too long ago, brisket wasn't even marketed because it was considered such a bad piece of beef. Brisket in grocery stores would be in the Select or Choice grades. Because brisket is a very tough meat that has to be cooked for a long time, avoid using Select grades of brisket. A Choice brisket will have more fat marbling and this will result in a juicier finished product. Also avoid buying any brisket, whole or flat, that has had most of the fat trimmed away. It may make sense to not be paying for brisket fat, but the fat is needed to help keep the meat moist during a long smoke.

There is another meat grade of brisket to consider. Certified Angus Beef brand was created in 1978 by the American Angus Association. Because of the decline in top quality beef, the USDA lowered the standards in their grading of beef carcasses in 1976. The Certified Angus Beef brand (also referred to as CAB) was created in response to the grading changes. Many stores and restaurants are selling "Angus Beef" under many names, but only meats with the CAB label meet the highest standards. The CAB brand is graded as Prime and the top third of Choice. We try to use only CAB meats in competition. When we've been unable to get CAB brisket, we don't score as well.

Brisket flats are best for slicing because the grain of the meat is oriented in a single direction. The point of the brisket is more suited to cubing or shredding. The point will have the most fat marbling and because of this it is more tender, juicy, and flavorful. The muscles in the point are much like that of a pork butt in that they are not oriented in the same direction. For presentation purposes in competition, brisket flats are turned in by teams because of how well it slices. If we cook a whole brisket, we try to include cubed pieces of the point to help act as a garnish and set our brisket apart from that of other teams.

Which briskets to buy out of the meat case can be a crapshoot at best. One tip is to use the limber test. Balance the brisket on your fist and see how much it droops down. The thinking is that if the brisket is limber uncooked, it may be more tender when cooked. Also don't buy the smallest or largest brisket—pick one in the middle weight range. Look for a brisket that has a good amount of fat marbling. Fat is flavor and creates a more moist meat when cooked. Whether you choose a whole brisket or a flat, the wisest choice would be to buy Certified Angus Beef brand.

HOW TO TRIM

If you purchase a brisket flat, no trimming is really necessary. A whole brisket though will require some of the fat to be trimmed. With the brisket laying fat side up, press down to find the hard areas of fat. These hardened fat areas will need to be trimmed off because they will not render during cooking. We trim only the hard fat away and leave at least a quarter of an inch of fat on top. The fat is needed to keep the meat moist during the long smoking.

Another area of fat that needs to be trimmed is along the sides between the flat and point. You'll notice that the point end is thicker than the flat end of the brisket. Also there is a line of hard fat on the point end separating it from the flat. Again this fat won't render and needs to be removed to make the point the same thickness as the flat. You may have to cut in a good bit to remove enough of the fat for the point to lay down. Some people don't remove any of this fat, but we think it helps the point and flat to cook in the same amount of time.

The flat has a very visible grain pattern before it is cooked. But once the brisket has been smoked, the bark on the outside of the meat makes it impossible to determine this direction. This grain direction is important to know to get the most tender slices. Brisket that is sliced across the grain and cooked until fork tender will easily tear apart and that is something the judges are looking for. Therefore, before cooking, cut off a small corner of the brisket and make the cut perpendicular to the grain of the meat. This squared corner will show you the grain direction after cooking. Don't throw away the cut off piece, cook it the same as the brisket and you'll have a tasty treat well before the brisket is done. This is done only on the flat of the brisket because the point doesn't have the same orientation of the muscles. The point also has more fat marbling and cooks up very tender. The point is best suited to be cubed or shredded. The point is what "burnt ends" are made from. The Arizona BBQ Association has some great pictures and instructions on trimming a brisket. Here's the URL...www.azbbqa.com/articles/brisket-trim.htm

HOW TO COOK

A brisket can be marinated for several days, but in competitions we have only about a half day to marinate. Marinating doesn't penetrate very deeply in a thick piece of meat, so we inject the marinade to even out the flavor. We try to make the brisket taste like beef, preferably, a "prime rib" flavor. Sounds funny, making beef taste like beef, but we feel that most people add flavors to brisket that don't complement the beef flavor.

The marinade that we inject is an "au jus" sauce consisting mainly of beef stock, Moore's Marinade, and other spices. One ingredient that may seem strange is the melted bacon grease. Because briskets have such a tendency to dry out, we thought why not add some fat in the injection. Bacon grease was a logical choice because it will also help add flavor to the beef.

Here's the exact recipe:

Au Jus Sauce

1 package of French's Au Jus Sauce seasoning
1 cup of Moore's Marinade
1 tbsp of Texas Pete Hot Sauce
2 cans of beef broth
3 tbsp of melted bacon grease
1 tbsp of mesquite liquid smoke

Make the French's Au Jus Sauce according to directions on the stove, except add the beef broth instead of water. Mix in the rest of the ingredients and simmer for fifteen minutes. Let cool before injecting.

Lay the brisket fat side up and inject through the fat cap every square inch. You want to insert the needle as far as you can without punching through the other side of the meat. Once the injections are completed, wrap the brisket in plastic wrap and store it on ice in a cooler. At a contest we usually get to allow the brisket to marinate for about six to ten hours before we start cooking.

We remove the brisket from the cooler about one hour before smoking. Unwrap the plastic from the brisket and place it on a table. We then apply a liberal coat of HomeBBQ Beef Rub on all surfaces and edges of the brisket. Even the small piece we cut off the flat, which was for checking the grain direction after cooking, gets coated with rub. After the rub, lay a piece of foil over the brisket to keep it covered while it warms up.

Our smoker takes about an hour to really heat up evenly so just before rubbing the brisket we will start the fire in the smoker. We cook brisket at 250°F. We use an even amount of oak and hickory to smoke brisket. Brisket requires a long smoke and it tends to act like a sponge soaking up smoke. Because of this, we don't recommend using mesquite to smoke brisket. Some of the best brisket is cooked out West on mesquite, but it is too easy to oversmoke the brisket if you don't have a lot of experience cooking with mesquite. Oversmoking any piece of meat will cause it to have a bitter taste.

Our smoker has an upper cooking grate and that is where we place the brisket (fat cap up) to start. We put the brisket opposite from the firebox end of the smoker because we want a more consistent temperature. The firebox end of most smokers will get too hot and the temperatures will fluctuate too much when adding fuel to the fire. Another thing we do is to place a disposable metal pan on the grate under the brisket. The pan needs to be large enough to hold the brisket. This pan catches any of the juices that flow from the meat and we will add this to the au jus sauce for more flavor.

After the brisket has smoked for four hours, we want to place it fat side down in the pan that has been catching the meat's juices. We then add just enough au jus sauce in the pan to bring it to a depth of one-quarter of an inch. The au jus should be brought to a simmer before adding to the pan. We now cook the brisket on the lower grate for the duration of the smoke. The juice in the pan will become our mop sauce to keep the brisket moist. The best tool for doing this would be a large turkey baster. We baste the brisket every hour with the au jus sauce until it is done.

Brisket cooks in about one to one and a half hours per pound, but there really isn't an exact temperature for finished brisket. We try to test the brisket after the temperature reaches 180°F. We test for tenderness with a really small meat thermometer probe. We check the meat again at 190° and then start checking every half hour. The place to check for tenderness and temperature is in the flat. The point of the brisket will always reach tenderness and temperature before the flat. Some people even separate the point from the flat when it is done. When brisket is done, the probe will slide in very easily. Brisket has to be cooked until it becomes "fork tender." Cooking brisket to a predetermined temperature every time won't always yield a tender piece of meat. Every brisket just has to be cooked until it "gives up the ghost," and becomes tender.

Once the brisket is tender, we cover the pan with foil and place it in a cooler to hold the temperature. Several folded towels placed over the pan help to hold in the heat. We can safely keep the brisket hot in the cooler for about four hours. About thirty minutes before we need to slice the brisket, we remove the pan from the cooler and slightly crack open the foil so that the meat can cool. This is called resting the meat. Beef needs to rest before slicing so that the juices can be reabsorbed back into the meat. Cutting any meat without letting it rest will allow the juices to spill out and the meat will become dry much quicker.

After the beef has rested, remove the brisket from the pan and place it on a cutting board with the fat side facing up. Don't discard the pan full of juices; we will use that later. Most of the fat on this side will have rendered away, but any remaining fat should be sliced or scraped off. We want to present the judges beautiful slices of brisket that have a nice crust, a deep smoke ring, and no fat visible. Now we flip the brisket over and begin slicing.

As we slice the brisket, we want to make sure we are cutting perpendicular, or across the grain of the flat. The notch we cut on the corner while trimming the brisket will help us determine how to slice. Slicing across the grain results in tender slices, while slicing with the grain creates slices that are very hard for a judge to pull apart. The judge will test the slice of brisket by determining how much force is needed to tear a slice in two. It should tear apart easily, but not fall apart when picked up.

The thickness of the brisket slices can affect the tenderness. Normally brisket should be sliced one-quarter inch thick, but if the brisket is a little tough, cut the slices a little thinner. If the brisket slices are falling apart when picked up, then cutting the slices thicker will help them hold together. If the brisket flat isn't very tall, cutting the slices at a slight bevel can create the illusion that the brisket flat was very thick. Think about a steak, a big, thick steak always looks better than a small thin one. It may taste the same, but it looks more appealing. Remember, the appearance score is given before the judge handles or tastes the meat. He or she bases the score totally on how the meat looks in the tray.

After the brisket is sliced, we dredge each slice through the pan of juices (it's a good idea to strain the au jus first). This does several things for us. First, brisket slices will dry out very quickly. So adding moisture helps keep the meat looking and tasting moist. This is important because from the time we turn in our meats to be judged, until a judge actually tastes the meat can be fifteen or twenty minutes. We have to do everything we can to keep the meat moist. Also the juices in the pan will give the brisket a boost in flavor. Cooking brisket for many hours can cook out some of the flavor. The au jus sauce helps to give it back. Some teams use a BBQ sauce on brisket, but we believe an au jus sauce complements without overpowering like some sauces can.

Placing the slices in the turn-in box is very critical. As we slice the brisket

we want to keep the slices in order if possible. This makes for a better presentation if the slices look uniform. The slices should be placed in the box starting from the back and fanning out, or shingling the slices so that some of the meat, smoke ring, and crust is visible on every slice. If the slices are too wide for the turn in box, you can place them at a diagonal or trim the ends of each slice. If you have cooked a whole brisket, take some of the point and cube it. These cubes can be placed in front of the brisket slices to help fill the tray. Some contests don't allow garnish, just meat in the turn-in box. But meat can also be legally used as a garnish. Another idea would be to shred or chop some of the brisket point and use it as garnish. You could even have sliced brisket, cubed, and shredded all in the same box. These are the things that can separate your box from all of the other teams.

Each contest determines the minimum amount of meat to turn in for judging. Some require enough for six judges, while others may require eight or ten judges be fed. We always try to turn in more than is required. A tray that is full of meat looks more appealing and it tells the judges we are confident in what we cooked, that we didn't just "cherry pick" the minimum number of slices needed from a average brisket. Also if a judge grabs a slice and another slice sticks to it, then the judge has to take both slices. If we put only the minimum number of slices, we could have a judge with no meat to score. So putting in extra meat ensures no judge will go without.

Normally each judging table has a table captain. The table captain may not be scoring, but it is a courtesy to put extra in for the captain. And we don't want to forget all of the volunteers who help to make the BBQ contests possible. These guys work awfully hard all weekend. Some contests have a "grazing table" set up to allow the volunteers to sample any leftover BBQ after the judging process. These volunteers are the real reason to turn in ample amounts of BBQ.

SMOKING A TURKEY

First step is buying a turkey. Buy a bird that is 13 lb. or less. A large smoked turkey will take too long to get out of the temperature danger zone (40 to 140°F) when using lower smoking temperatures. We prefer Butterball turkey because the breast meat has been deep basted to increase moisture and flavor. Butterball turkeys that are fresh, not frozen, are not basted. So we prefer the frozen ones because of this. Also, a frozen turkey can be bought well ahead of the time needed to cook, not so with fresh turkey.

A frozen turkey needs to be thawed in the refrigerator, not in the kitchen sink or on the countertop. Thawing a 10-13 lb. turkey may take up to three or four days in the refrigerator. Check the temperature setting on your appliance and raise the temp setting if needed but, remember, the turkey should always be kept well below 40° to avoid spoiling.

All right, besides the turkey, you will need a sweet onion, an orange, two red apples, and three stalks of celery. We will also use extra virgin olive oil to help the skin brown and cook evenly. The oil will also act as a binder for the rub applied.

After removing the neck and giblets from the bird, wash with cold water. Then use paper towels to dry the turkey skin. Drying the skin will help the olive oil coat evenly and this will make the smoked turkey's skin more evenly colored when done. Now we can coat the turkey with the olive oil. Rub the olive oil into the skin and make sure to apply some inside the cavity of the bird.

Next we cut up the onion, apples, orange, and celery. Stuff the cavity with these ingredients, using as much as you can fit into the turkey. This is not a stuffing that you would want to eat. The purpose of this stuffing is to help add moisture and flavor to the turkey. You could go a step further and pour a can of Coke into the cavity. This adds a unique flavor and can further help in the moisture level of the turkey.

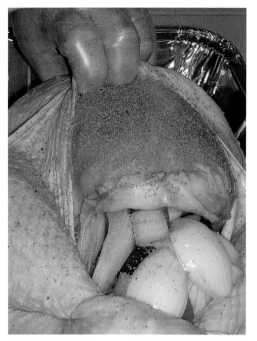

Now it's time to rub the turkey. I use Paula Deen's spices for my rub. It is two teaspoons of each of these seasonings: Butt Massage, Seasoned Salt, and House Seasoning. The six teaspoons of seasoning are added to one cup of brown sugar for the finished rub. You can just substitute your favorite rub instead of Paula Deen's spices. The rub is applied first under the skin on the breast. Work your fingers under the skin and then pull it back far enough to coat the breast meat well. Then cover the entire bird with the rub, gently rubbing it into the olive oil on the skin.

You could cook the smoked turkey directly on the smoker's cooking grate, but with any poultry cooked on a smoker or a grill, the fat rendering out can cause some mighty big flare-ups. We use a wire rack inside of a large disposable aluminum pan. The pan catches all of the juices cooking from the turkey, which can be used to baste the turkey. And the wire rack keeps the bird from sitting in the meat juices. The turkey is placed on the wire rack with the breast side facing up during the entire smoking process.

Most slow cooked barbeque is cooked at 250°F or less. But for smoked turkey we jump the smoker temperature up to 325°F. Cooking at higher temps will help to conserve moisture in the meat and also get the turkey out of the danger zone more quickly. A 10–13 lb. bird should take no more than four to four and a half hours at 325°F. The turkey will be done when the temperature in the thigh reaches 180°F. The temperature probe should be placed in the thickest part of the thigh, making sure not to touch any bones. Another doneness test is to grab the drumstick and give it a wiggle. If

it feels like it will pull loose easily from the body of the turkey, then the bird is probably done. Also check that the meat juices flow clear when piercing the thigh with a fork.

After about an hour of smoking the turkey with a combination of hickory and apple wood pellets, check to see how the skin looks. If any area appears to be getting too brown, loosely covering that area with foil will help to prevent burning. About the two-hour mark of cooking, loosely cover the breasts to keep them from cooking faster than the legs and thigh meat. After the three-hour mark you can baste the turkey with melted butter every half hour until done. This will help to keep the skin from drying out and make the turkey a more golden brown color.

Now you may be asking why didn't you brine the turkey or at least inject the turkey? I just find with the Butterball turkey you don't have to do all of that to get a great finished product. The turkey will be moist and flavorful without injections and brines. It's really easy to get carried away with flavors on turkey. This recipe keeps it fairly simple and you don't have to start prepping the turkey days before cooking.

One last thing about carving turkey—and this applies to all turkey no matter how it is cooked. A cold turkey carves much better than a hot turkey, so it is better to cook the turkey the day before you plan to serve it. Refrigerate it overnight and slice away the next day. The slices can be easily warmed in a foil-covered pan in the oven.

TRIMMING SPARERIBS ST. LOUIS STYLE

This is how I cut spareribs St. Louis style. This cut involves removing the skirt meat on the back side (bone side) of the slab and also cutting off the brisket or what is also known as rib tips. Everything we cut off will still be cooked; nothing goes to waste! To do these cuts you'll need a cutting board, sharp boning or large knife, and several paper towels.

First turn the slab of ribs meat side down so that you can see the skirt or flap of meat on the bone side. Sometimes you'll find this has already been removed by the butcher and you can skip this step.

Figure 1: An untrimmed slab of pork spareribs.

Simply grab the skirt meat and as you lift up on it, cut it away from the slab as close as possible without exposing the bones (see Fig. 2). I always cook the skirt meat using the same rub for the ribs. The skirt meat will cook up quickly and is a "sweet treat" for the cook! One other thing you can do to the skirt meat is remove the membrane on the back of it. This will make the skirt piece more tender but it is not absolutely necessary.

Figure 2: Removing the skirt meat from bone side.

Next step is to flip the rib meat side up and remove the brisket (rib tips). This is where a good knife is needed. The object here is to cut the slab into a uniform width so that the ribs cook more evenly (see Fig. 3). Start at the end that has the largest bones. Find where the joints are between the rib bones and the brisket. You want to cut right thru these joints or you'll have a tough time cutting through bones. Also notice how the rib bones change about half to two-thirds of the way down the slab. You will be cutting through the joints on about the first five to seven ribs. The last half or third of the slab will consist of bones that are more like cartilage. When you get to these bones, just continue to cut the slab at the same width as you cut the first bones. This will give you a uniform rack of ribs. At this point your spareribs will resemble a slab of baby backs.

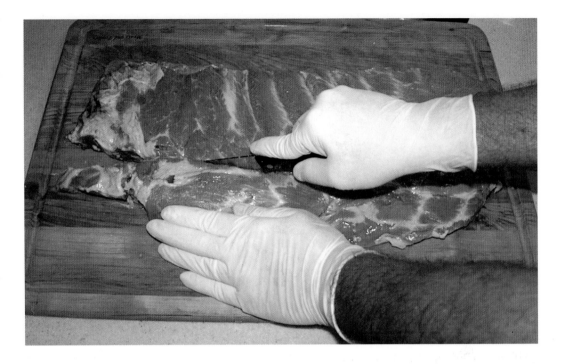

Figure 3: Trimming away the brisket.

The last step to our St. Louis-style ribs is removal of the membrane on the bone side. Removing the membrane makes for a more tender rib and also allows more flavor from smoke and rub to penetrate. Start at the large bone end and gently try to pry the membrane up with your knife (see Fig. 4). A butter knife actually works better than a sharp knife at prying up the membrane.

Once you lift the edge of the membrane, you'll notice what appears to be another membrane layer. Do not remove it. The second membrane is needed to hold the ribs together.

After you get the membrane started, work your finger under the top membrane until you have it pulled loose on the first rib bone. Now you can use the paper towels. The membrane is hard to hold onto, but you can get a good grip with the paper towels. Holding the slab down with one hand, begin pulling the membrane back away. As you get some of the membrane pulled off, roll it around the paper towel so that you can pull on the membrane closer to the ribs. This will help keep the membrane from tearing. If it does tear, just try to pry it up again, grip with towels, and continue removing until all of the membrane is off.

Figure 4: Prying up the membrane.

Figure 5: Pulling off membrane.

In Fig. 6, the top piece of meat is the skirt that was cut off first. The bottom piece is the brisket or rib tips, and the middle is the rack of St. Louis-style spareribs.

Figure 6: The finished pieces from St Louis Style cuts.

Figure 7: St Louis Style ribs, rubbed *& ready to cook!*

BARBECUE RECIPE SCIENCE

There's a whole lot of "science" behind what makes good slow-smoked barbecue recipes develop their flavor, tenderness, appearance, and moisture content. So, let's take a few of the reactions and try to explain the science behind them...

BROWNING...

This is also called the Maillard reaction and is named after the French scientist Louis Camille Maillard. It is a reaction between amino acids on the meat's surface and sugars in the presence of heat. The Maillard reaction and the smoke introduced to the meat's surface give barbecue its characteristic "bark." Usually, well-smoked barbecue has a crust that is black in color, suggesting the Maillard reaction on overdrive. Don't worry...this is a good thing. Most people love the "bark" on a properly cooked Boston butt or brisket.

SEARING...

Most barbecue pit masters do not sear their meat before smoking. Searing meat is cooking it for very short amounts of time in an attempt to seal in the juices. Scientific tests have been performed that weigh two identical pieces of meat before and after cooking. One being seared and the other not. Test results show that the seared piece of meat lost more moisture than the meat not seared. If searing is done properly, it will improve the flavor due to the Maillard reaction, but it will probably not improve juiciness very much. This one is extremely controversial though. Many chefs swear by "searing in the juices." Maybe there is something to it because after reading the paragraph on resting, you'll understand how the muscle fibers contract when heated and push the juices to the center of the meat.

THE SMOKE RING...

The smoke ring is important for aesthetic reasons, but as far as flavor is concerned, it contributes none. The smoke ring is just a chemical reaction between nitrogen dioxide and the amino acids in the meat, which produce a pink color. Nitrogen dioxide is produced when wood is burned at temperatures exceeding 600°F. Note this is in the firebox and not your cooking chamber. The smoke ring really has nothing to do with smoke at all. The smoke will impart its flavor to the surface of the meat independent of the smoke ring reaction. Interestingly enough, gas grills do produce nitrogen dioxide. Some sawdust-burning smokers that combust at lower temperatures do not produce nitrogen dioxide. Of course, ovens do not produce smoke rings, but what kind of jackass would cook barbecue in an oven anyway!? Note that in barbecue competitions, some judges do not know these facts; they think the smoke ring is caused by smoke and they take that as a sign of properly smoked meats—especially brisket. So producing a good smoke ring is important.

RESTING...

I can't say this loudly enough...make sure you properly rest your meat before slicing or pulling! As the outside muscle fibers in the meat heat up, they contract and push the moisture to the center of the meat. If you pull a piece of meat off the fire and set it on a cutting board, you'll see that some of the juices will naturally run out. If you cut the meat prematurely, about twice as much will run out. And you wonder why your brisket is so dry! Let the meat rest at room temperature. If it is too cold outside, wrap it in aluminum foil and let it rest that way. Do not put it in the refrigerator or icebox to rest. Let chicken and ribs rest for fifteen minutes and butts and brisket for thirty minutes. Of course, always slice your brisket against the grain. And now would be a good time to tell you...stop poking holes in your meat! Every time you poke a hole in your meat, you can literally see the juices flow out! How stupid is that!? Poke it once with a meat thermometer and leave the probe in. Otherwise, use your hands or tongs to move your meat around. Injecting is a whole different story. Injections are done before cooking and they generally introduce a whole lot more moisture than they let out. Some of the moisture will leak out, but it's sort of an offset, the benefit being the introduction of more flavors to the center of the meat. Your meat probably will not be juicier, but it may improve the taste a bit.

BOILING POINT OF WATER...

Did you ever notice that good, juicy barbecue is slowly cooked near the boiling point of water? This way, the water does not evaporate too fast and stays in and on the meat longer—basting the meat surface and keeping it moist inside and out. The slow and low temperature also allows the collagen in the muscle fibers to break down over time to produce tenderness. The boiling point of water is 212°F, for those pit masters who didn't know. But that's only at sea level. As you go up in altitude, the atmospheric pressure goes down and the boiling point of water drops. At 1,000 feet, it's 210°F. At 2,500 feet, it's 207°F. At 4,000 feet, it's 204°F. And at 6,000 feet, it's only 201°F. That's why it takes so long to boil an egg in the mountains. So...instead of cooking at 225°F at an elevation of 5,000 feet, maybe try 215°F and just cook it a little longer. That way all your juices will not evaporate too fast.

FOILING...

I know none of you would ever do this in a million years, but have you ever had boiled ribs? They are usually fall off the bone tender. You have to slather on a whole lot of barbecue sauce to get any taste out of them, but that's beside the point. The point is they are cooked at exactly the proper temperature (212°F) and the "tenderness" result is pretty good. When you cook ribs on a smoker and you use the foiling technique, you are essentially steaming the ribs. Steam is usually about the same temperature as boiling water unless it is under high pressure or reheated. The result is something similar to boiled ribs, but you don't lose as much of the flavor. Properly used for short amounts of time, it's an effective technique to produce tender ribs, butts, and brisket.

WEATHER...

Also keep an eye on your weather. If it's cold outside, of course you'll need a hotter fire to maintain the proper temperature in your cooking chamber. Rain dropping on your smoker and evaporating will transport a lot of heat away from your smoker. So, if you see rain, build up your fire a bit and maybe open the vent a little more. On hot dry days, you'll probably want a slightly lower temperature in your cooker so you don't evaporate the basting moisture too much. Conversely, on very humid days, you can probably get away with a somewhat hotter temperature.

COLLAGEN, PROTEIN, AND FAT

Just exactly what happens when you are cooking barbecue? And when I say "cooking barbecue," I mean slow smoking barbecue—not grilling directly over high heat. First of all... meat is made up of mostly protein muscle fibers held together with collagen strands along with a little bit of fat. Three things happen when you apply TOO MUCH heat to meat...

collagen triple helix

- Some of the collagen liquefies and turns into gelatin. This process starts when the meat temperature is around 140°F.

- Some of the fat also starts to melt at around 140°F.

- Note: melting collagen and fat is a slow process, so applying too much heat for short times will only melt some of the collagen and fat.

- Too much heat will cause the muscle proteins to contract, curl, and squeeze out the natural juices mixed with the liquefied collagen and fat. The result is dry, tough meat. Just think about what happens when you slap a steak on a hot grill... it firms up and the juices start to flow out. Cook it "well done" and you basically get shoe leather.

Cooking barbecue (slow smoking) is different because of the lower heat involved. Here's what happens when meat is cooked at a lower temperature for a long time...

- The process of liquefying collagen and turning it into gelatin is a slow process. It does not happen instantly when the meat temperature hits 140°F. It takes time—low and slow. So the longer you hold the meat temperature above 140°F, the more collagen will turn into gelatin.

- Same thing with the melting of the fat—it takes time.

- The protein muscle fibers start to relax and the juices are absorbed rather than squeezed out. Cooking barbecue in this low and slow fashion results in tender, succulent meats.

If you are experienced at cooking barbecue, you know about the "barbecue plateau" where your meat tends to get stuck at a certain temperature (around

165°F) and stay there. An experienced pit master knows this is when all the "good stuff" is happening...your collagen strands are unwinding, your fat is melting, and your muscle proteins are slowly relaxing instead of seizing up. So...the "barbecue plateau" is a good thing. When your internal meat temperatures start to rise after the plateau, you need to start checking for doneness because any further cooking will tend to dry out your meat.

BBQ COMPETITIONS

In the last couple of years the number of BBQ contests has expanded rapidly. The Kansas City Barbeque Society has gone from 100 members in 1988 to 1400 in 1993 to over 10,000 members in 2008. And they sanction over 300 events every year. BBQ contests are not just limited to the South and Midwest anymore, as barbecue associations have sprung up in the Northeast and on the West Coast. As cities across America increasingly look to draw guests into their towns with festivals and events, we will only see an ever-increasing number of competitions to complement these events. The best way to find a contest near you is to go to the section on Barbecue Associations, visit the Web site of the association in your area, and then look at a calendar of events or contest schedule. The www.barbecuenews.com Web site has the best list of contests on one Web site.

If you've never competed before, but think you might be interested in doing so, then attending a contest as a spectator is a great way to learn. Most contests last from Friday to Saturday evening. Teams begin setting up early Friday morning preparing to cook through the night. By the afternoon most teams will have their meats prepped and iced down. This is a good time to visit with the teams and ask questions. You will easily find people willing to answer your questions about competing and barbecue in general.

Visiting a contest will also let you get a glimpse of just about every type of smoker available. Cooks won't hesitate to talk about cookers and why they think theirs is the best. You will usually see cookers ranging from trash cans to rigs costing tens of thousands of dollars. Just remember that it's the cook not the cooker. We know of many teams that win consistently on smokers that cost less than $200!

Saturday is also a good day to view a contest. If you visited the contest on Friday, you'll quickly notice that most teams are much more serious on Saturday than they were the night before. Friday at a contest is more like a party atmosphere. It's time for teams to visit with old friends on other teams and just generally relax for a while. Saturday is a different story. Teams are critically watching their smokers and making final preparations to turn in their entries. Most teams won't mind if you watch as they work on Saturday. But it's best to be respectful of the teams and avoid entering their assigned cook space, unless they invite you, of course.

HOW CONTESTS ARE USUALLY CONDUCTED

Most contests allow teams to begin setting up early Friday morning. First thing is to find the check-in point or the person responsible for checking teams into the contest area. They will show you to your assigned site and can answer any questions about the contest area. The very next thing to do, even before the unpacking really begins, is to have your contest meats inspected. Contests don't allow any seasoning or marinating of the meats before they are inspected so it is usually best to get this done quickly. But you can pre-trim and thoroughly wash any meats at home. This saves valuable time so that meat can be injected and begin marinating as soon as possible.

Once on your site, you want to find the electrical and water hookups. In our case, we determine how and where we want to set our smoker and canopy and position those first. We then unpack all of our equipment and get it set up in place. We have our own sink with cabinet that we set up under the canopy. Our table for prepping meats also must be set up under the canopy. After everything has been unloaded, we pull the meats from coolers to begin injecting and marinating. The meats then go back in the cooler until ready to smoke. This is usually the downtime at a contest where everyone has a chance to visit and talk with each other for a while.

The contest organizers will usually have a cooks' meeting around 5:00 or 6:00 in the evening on Friday. At least one member from each team is required to attend the meeting. This is when all the rules should be covered and if there any questions, now is the time to ask them. You'll get a schedule of turn-in times and you'll also receive the turn-in trays.

The trays will have your assigned number on them—they will not have your team name on them. Most contests use a double-blind numbering system. When you turn in your tray for judging, another number will be taped over your original number. This way nobody knows which entry is being judged until after the judging and the numbers are removed.

You have to be very careful and make sure your turn-in trays don't get damaged. It is a good idea to have them put up out of sight and harm's way until each meat is ready to be turned in for judging. The trays have to be perfectly clean without any marks to avoid violating the rules of marking the turn in tray.

Any marking of the trays can be grounds for disqualification. And you won't get back entry fees!

After the cooks' meeting, the contest organization usually gives a cooks' supper. Most will give up to five dinners per team before they begin charging for additional meals. This is a good time to meet many new friends before the cooking begins. Once the smokers get going, everyone begins to concentrate on the competition and the opportunities for fellowship with others stop for a while. However, if you have teams cooking near you, there is always plenty of time to sit and talk as you watch the coals glow and the stars shine above. Just remember to focus on what your smoker is doing.

We usually write out what steps will be done during the smoking process. Every step of the contest is listed with a time. This way, all of us on the team know when and what is going to happen. A list like this also helps when you cook all night with little sleep. It's easy to forget a critical step when fatigued. Setting a cooking time line also ensures that you will allow enough time to properly cook the meat (it would be a good idea to do this in your backyard too). We try to figure how long it will take to cook each meat and then allow some extra time. If the meat gets done early, it can be wrapped in aluminum foil and placed in a hot cooler to hold its temperature until turn-in time. Meats can be held in a cooler for many hours without much heat loss.

On Saturday, the meats are turned in at the specified times. There is usually a ten-minute window (five minutes before and up to five minutes after specified time) for each turn-in. Most contests start with chicken at eleven o'clock and then follow with ribs a half hour to one hour later. Pork turn-in follows ribs, followed by brisket.

There will be a designated place to take the turn-in tray for judging and you should verify the location at the cooks' meeting. It's a good idea to have a designated person to turn in the trays. We aim for an early turn in—that way if we have any problems there will be enough time to correct them. You don't want to be even a second late because they have the right to refuse your entry. An official time is always given at the cooks' meeting and it's a good idea to synchronize someone's watch or a clock to the official time.

Once everything is turned in, it's time to take a breather and relax before having to break down the cook site. The awards ceremony is held several hours after the last turn-in, and as we reflect back on what we cooked there is the anticipation of how well we will score.

We try to get everything cleaned and packed up before heading off to the awards ceremony. Some contests ask you not to pack up before the awards are announced, but you can still pack all your boxes and tidy up. Just leave the canopy and smoker out until the end.

BBQ ASSOCIATIONS

BBQ contests fall into two categories, sanctioned and non-sanctioned. Associations around the country put on contests that follow their rules for competing and judging. These are sanctioned contests. Two of the best-known sanctioned contests are Memphis in May and the American Royal.

MEMPHIS BARBECUE ASSOCIATION
WWW.MEMPHISINMAY.ORG
WWW.MBNBBQ.COM

Memphis in May is an invitational contest sanctioned by the Memphis BBQ Association (MBA). MBA contests are pork only. Teams compete in pork ribs (loin or spareribs), pork shoulder (consists of Boston butt and the picnic ham together), and whole hog. One aspect unique to MBA is that you don't have to cook in all three categories to win the Grand Champion title at a contest. The team that has the highest score in any one of the three categories wins the title of Grand Champion and gets invited to cook at Memphis in May. If the winning team already has an invite, the next team in the standings is invited. This is called a pass down and late in the year when many teams have already won an invitation, it could be the fourth- or fifth-place team that wins an invitation.

MBA contests also differ in the judging process. Teams turn in blind judging boxes and are scored on presentation, taste, and tenderness. But teams are also judged at their cook site by at least three judges. The teams explain to the judges how and why they cook and allow the judges to sample the teams' barbecue. The on-site judging doesn't take long, but three judges visit for each pork category entered. If you are lucky enough to make it to the finals (top three in each category), there is another round of on-site judging. Note: MIM has stopped sanctioning contests so they can concentrate on the Memphis in May contest and has turned over contest sanctioning to the Memphis Barbecue Network at www.mbnbbq.com.

KANSAS CITY BBQ SOCIETY (KCBS) WWW.KCBS.US

The American Royal, held in Kansas City, Missouri, each year, is sanctioned by the Kansas City Barbecue Society (KCBS). The KCBS has grown into the largest sanctioning body in the world. The last few years have seen a dramatic increase in KCBS contests and last year they sanctioned more than 300 events. The American Royal has grown into a huge contest with more than 550 teams competing in 2005.

In a KCBS contest, teams compete in chicken, pork, ribs, and brisket. The scores in each category are added together to determine the overall Grand Champion. A team has to cook in all four meat categories to have a chance at the Grand Champion title. The team with the second-highest score is awarded Reserve Grand Champion.

KCBS judges each entry for presentation, taste, and tenderness. Taste is worth twice as much as tenderness, and tenderness is worth twice as much as presentation. The judging is blind, meaning that the judges don't know which team they are evaluating. Each team is scored by six judges. The lowest score is dropped from a team's total score. Consider joining the KCBS as a member and you'll receive their excellent barbecue newspaper...*The Kansas City BullSheet*.

FLORIDA BBQ ASSOCIATION WWW.FLBBQ.ORG

The FBA holds contests mostly in Florida, but has begun expanding into Georgia, Alabama, and Tennessee. Rules are very close to KCBS except no garnish is allowed. You should also check out the *National Barbecue News* Web site and consider subscribing. This is by far the best source of BBQ information available. In addition to the great articles and contest results, there are plenty of advertisers selling those hard-to find-items that you may want. Their Web site contains a wealth of free information, BBQ forums, and their calendar of events showing you where you can enter or visit your next competition...www.barbecuenews.com.

Here is a list of all known BBQ Associations and a list of BBQ competitions in their area. Information is usually on a page like "calendar of events."

The National Barbecue News – www.barbecuenews.com (While not an association, they have one of the most comprehensive lists of BBQ contests available.)

Kansas City Barbecue Society – www.kcbs.us
Florida Barbecue Association – www.flbbq.org
National Barbecue Association – www.nbbqa.org
California Barbecue Association - www.cbbqa.com
Memphis Barbecue Association — www.memphisinmay.org
Memphis Barbecue Network – www.mbnbbq.com
New England Barbecue Society – www.nebs.org
Lone Star Barbecue Society – www.lonestarbarbecue.com
Central Texas Barbecue Association – www.ctbahome.com
Texas Gulf Coast Barbecue Cooker's Association – www.tgcbca.org
South Carolina Barbecue Association – www.scbarbeque.com
North Carolina Barbecue Society – www.ncbbqsociety.com
Arizona Barbecue Association – www.azbbqa.com
Greater Omaha Barbecue Society – www.gobs.org
Iowa Barbecue Society – www.iabbq.org
Mid Atlantic Barbecue Association – www.mabbqa.com
Pacific Northwest Barbecue Association – www.pnwba.com
Utah BBQ Association – www.utahbbq.org
Canadian Barbecue Association – www.canadianbarbecueassociation.com
International Barbecue Cookers Association – www.ibcabbq.org
Rocky Mountain BBQ Association – www.rmbbqa.com
Georgia Barbecue Association - www.georgiabarbecueassociation.com

Note: if you can't find a contest near you in the list above, just type one of the following terms into www.google.com...

yourstate barbecue contest
yourstate barbecue association
yourstate barbecue society
yourstate barbecue competition

FUN OF COMPETING

BBQ contests are a whole lot of fun. Sure...there are some very serious players, but nearly all of them are friendly and I'll bet you a dollar that they would not be out there competing every other weekend if it were not for the camaraderie. BBQ cooking teams are basically very friendly, down-to-earth competitive people. There's plenty of time for walking around and saying hey to all your fellow competitors and friends. Some of them get a little crazy at times too...

There is usually a cooks' meeting on Friday night, which almost always includes a big dinner for everyone (usually not BBQ though). There are also other competitions throughout the weekend that are great fun like Kids Q, pie contests, anything but Q, chili cookoffs, sauce competitions, and "backyard" competitions for the amateurs. My mom had a blast competing in the apple pie contest in Douglas, Georgia (www.nationalbbqfestival.com). She came in eighth place out of fifty and got a ribbon...

I had a good time in the sauce contest in Pooler, Georgia, and won second place and a huge trophy...

Barnsville, Georgia, BBQ and Blues Festival
April 2006
Reserve Grand Champions

There's nothing more fun than doing really well in a BBQ Contest! Using the exact same techniques detailed in this book, we placed first in chicken, second in ribs, and second in pork. We also came in second place overall and were Reserve Grand Champions, winning $1,300 in prize money and four nice trophies. *Now that's what I call fun!*

If you really want to go see a crazy BBQ competition, go to the Big Pig Jig in Vienna, Georgia (www.bigpigjig.com). These competitors rent out these small twenty-by-twenty-foot or twenty-by-forty-foot sites every year and they build these huge structures that they just leave there until next year. They build saloons, lounge areas, and three- and four-story towers. This is one fun and crazy contest! And one thing I forgot to mention...they usually have a great band that plays for the contestants and visitors on Saturday afternoon just before the announcement of the winners...

WHAT YOU NEED TO GET STARTED

- Smoker – One large smoker or several smaller models may be needed to cook the required meats in a competition. Some teams use as many as four Weber Smokey Mountain Smokers to cook chicken, ribs, butts, and brisket.

- Canopy – An EZ-Up-style canopy or similar. A ten-by-ten-foot canopy is the best size. It is best that the footprint of the canopy is the same as the canopy size. Some canopies have poles that flare out. It's a good idea to purchase the canopy sides if available. The sides will help on windy, rainy, or cold days.

- Tables – Need a table for preparing meats. The table should be NSF approved (has to do with surfaces that don't allow food particles to become trapped). Table should be at least thirty-six inches tall. A short table can be extended higher by adding lengths of PVC pipe to each leg.

- Coolers – Will need two or three large coolers. At least one cooler for uncooked meats and the other for food and beverages.

- Chimney– Charcoal chimney needed to burn charcoal down to coals.

- Power cords – Need at least 150 feet of heavy gauge electrical cord. May need several smaller cords and a multiple outlet plug.

- Lights – Portable lights to illuminate the canopy and smoker areas.

- Water hose – Need at least one hundred feet of water hose. Also need a hose end sprayer and a Y connect to split water to two hoses.

- Sink – Preferable to have a sink for washing hands and pans, but a couple of dishpans will also work. Our sink has a drain hose and we sometimes have to use one of those five-gallon filtered water bottles to hold the drain water if there is no place to run the drain hose to. You can also buy one of those waste water tanks that are used on small campers—they are nice because they have wheels.

- Thermometer – Needed to know internal temperature of meat. An instant read digital thermometer is good, but a better choice is an electronic unit with a wired temperature probe and maybe even a remote wireless module with alarms and timers. This allows meat to be monitored without opening smoker.

- Utensils – Good sharp knives, spatulas, basting brushes, tongs, measuring cups and spoons, plastic spray bottles, sauce mop, cutting board, marinade injector, shakers for rubs.

- Other – Heavy-duty aluminum foil, plastic wrap, large ziplock bags, paper towels, cloth dishtowels.

- Cleaners – Dishwashing soap (anti-bacterial) and hand washing soap (also anti-bacterial).

- Chlorine bleach is needed as a disinfectant. Mix one cap of bleach with one gallon of water and store in a spray bottle. Make sure bottle is labeled. Some people prefer to use just straight vinegar for disinfecting cutting board surfaces.

BBQ PACKING LIST

☐ Three-way power cord adaptors
☐ Aprons
☐ Ash bucket, metal
☐ Ash scoop/shovel
☐ Axe or hatchet for splitting wood
☐ BBQ sauces
☐ Beer or other drinks
☐ Bleach solution or vinegar for disinfecting surfaces
☐ Brushes and mops for slathering
☐ Canopy (ten by ten)
☐ Chairs
☐ Charcoal chimney
☐ Cloth towels/rags
☐ Cutting boards
☐ Decorative lights
☐ Dishpan
☐ Dish soap
☐ Drip pan for smoker
☐ Duct tape
☐ Electrical cords
☐ Fire starters
☐ Food, snacks, etc.
☐ Garden Hose, one hundred feet
☐ Grill cleaner brush
☐ Grill spatula and tongs
☐ Hose sprayer
☐ Ice (also available at contests)
☐ Ice chests
☐ Injection syringes
☐ Jackets
☐ Knife sharpener
☐ Knives
☐ Lights, clamp on
☐ Lights, halogen
☐ Lump charcoal
☐ Matches or lighter

- ☐ Meat cleavers
- ☐ Meat hook
- ☐ Oven thermometers and meat thermometer
- ☐ Paper towels
- ☐ Plastic wrap (high temp.)
- ☐ Pliers, screwdriver, and other tools
- ☐ Pots and pans
- ☐ Propane tank and brush burner for starting fire
- ☐ Rubber gloves, latex for handling food
- ☐ Rubber mitts for handling meat on smoker
- ☐ Rubs
- ☐ Sleeping bags
- ☐ Sleeping cots
- ☐ Spray bottles for apple juice, etc.
- ☐ Squeeze bottles
- ☐ Steel knife sharpener
- ☐ Tablecloth, vinyl
- ☐ Tent, camper, or RV for sleeping in
- ☐ Timers
- ☐ Tinfoil (heavy duty)
- ☐ Trash bags
- ☐ Trophies and awards
- ☐ Y Valve for water hose hookup
- ☐ Ziplock one-gallon bags
- ☐ Ziplock two-gallon bags

RESOURCE PAGE

OUR MONTHLY NEWSLETTERS – WWW.BBQSUCCESS.COM

Don't forget about our monthly newsletter Web site! It's a wealth of information! Lots of great information like how to smoke a brisket Texas style, Kansas City ribs, white sauces, Maverick digital remote thermometers, a chicken recipe that won a $1,000 prize, and much more! Also visit our blog where we post all your questions and answers—this is a great resource for all those hard-to-find answers to your BBQ problems...www.bbq-book.com/blog.

BIG GREEN EGGS – WWW.BIGGREENEGG.COM

These are ceramic cookers. Very fuel efficient and create a moist cooking environment. You'll see them referred to on the internet as BGEs. They are sold thru a dealer network. See their Web site for a dealer near you.

MAVERICK DIGITAL REMOTE THERMOMETERS – WWW.BBQ-BOOK.BIZ

You got to have one of these to slow smoke right. Not only will it let you keep track of the internal temperature of your meat, but it has a second probe so you can easily keep track of the temperature inside your cooking chamber AT THE GRATE. All wirelessly!

CERTIFIED ANGUS BEEF –
WWW.CERTIFIEDANGUSBEEF.COM

This is great site that tells about the CAB programs. On this site, you can find the nearest retailer of Certified Angus Beef.

COOKSHACK – WWW.COOKSHACK.COM

A manufacturer of residential and commercial smokers. Cookshack sells a line of electric smokers that are great for home use. They also sell a smoker popular in competitions, the Fast Eddy by Cookshack (FEC 100). This cooker uses all wood pellets and is as easy to cook on as an oven. The FEC smokers are available in our BBQ Store at www.bbq-book.biz. We purchase the Spicy Chicken Rub and the Spicy BBQ Sauce Mix from these guys (remember—the BBQ sauce mix is what we use for our dry rub). Great stuff!

DURAFLAME – WWW.DURAFLAME.COM

Maker of charcoal briquettes and lump charcoal. Haven't been able to find their lump charcoal, but I have used the Hardwood Charcoal Briquets and they were great. I did a short review of them in my monthly newsletter. Site has a store locater search.

HOMEBBQ – WWW.HOMEBBQ.COM

A championship winning barbecue team from Florida that sells their rubs and sauces. We use their Rib Rub and Beef Rub for brisket. They also have a forum where you can find a lot of BBQ info.

LANG SMOKERS – WWW.PIGROAST.COM

Ben Lang of Nahunta, Georgia, makes one of the best offset-style smokers. His smokers use a reverse flow plate to even out the cooking temperatures and this plate allows you to cook without turning the meat, which cooks evenly on both sides.

NAKED WHIZ – WWW.NAKEDWHIZ.COM

No this isn't a naked site! This guy has the best reviews of all of the brands of lump charcoal on the market. His site has some really cool info that you won't find anywhere on the Web.

NATIONAL BARBECUE NEWS – WWW.BARBECUENEWS.COM

A monthly barbecue newspaper that all serious barbecue people must have. Great barbecue columns, recipes, contest news, as well as reviews of books, videos, and barbecue products. The National Barbecue News also has one of the best BBQ forums on the Web. They also host the National Barbecue Festival in Douglas, Georgia, the first of November each year. This is where the Best of the Best compete.

OLE RAY'S SAUCES – WWW.OLERAYSSAUCES.COM

Ray Green makes some of the best sauces. His sauces continually win awards at sauce contests. We love and use his Apple/Cinnamon Sauce on ribs and pork. He has many sauces to choose from and they're all GOOD!

BIG BOB GIBSON'S – WWW.BIGBOBGIBSONBBQ.COM

We use his sauce on our pork butts. He must know what he is doing, as he participates on the BBQ competition circuit and places high in just about every contest he enters. His sauces are also available in most grocery stores.

TRAEGER PELLET SMOKERS – WWW.TRAEGERINDUSTRIES.COM

We replaced our Lang offset smoker last year with a few Traeger Lil' Tex pellet smokers and a Cookshack FEC100. The pellet smoker is a lot easier to operate and maintains a more consistent temperature.

PRIMO GRILLS – WWW.PRIMOGRILL.COM

These cookers are made in Atlanta, Georgia. The grills are made of ceramics like the Big Green Eggs. Their largest smoker is oval shaped and has good capacity.

STUMP'S SMOKERS – WWW.STUMPSSMOKERS.COM

Walter "Stump" McDowell builds one great smoker. His smokers are insulated so they are very fuel efficient. Stump's newest smokers have a gravity feed charcoal hopper. This allows the user to load the hopper full of charcoal and gravity feeds the coals down into the firebox as needed. With these units you can cook all night and never have to add fuel. Many teams are using Stump's Smokers and winning grand championships.

SOUTHERN YANKEE BBQ – WWW.SYBBQ.COM

Southern Yankee has a complete line of every type of BBQ smoker you can imagine. They specialize in concession-type rigs.

THE BBQ FORUM – WWW.THEBBQFORUM.COM

This is probably the most informative BBQ site on the Web. Ray Basso moderates the forum well and many competition teams across the country post here. If you have a BBQ question, you can search the archived section and find a quick answer. There's a ton of BBQ information on the BBQ Forum.

MORE GREAT BBQ BOOKS...

(available at www.bbq-book.biz)

Barbecue Secrets Revealed – Amazing Secret Finally Revealed by Retired Kentucky Restaurant Owner Eliminates All Guesswork...And Makes Cooking Up "Practically Addictive" Barbecue Simple! Now you can learn to make everything you grill or barbecue 100% more flavorful almost overnight, getting the perfect results you could only dream of before...while grilling steak after steak, and rib after rib, exactly how you want it, as consistent as clockwork...and, if you're like most barbecuers, turning heads at your very next BBQ! by Randy Pryor.

Super Secrets of Throwing a Kickass BBQ by Gef Smith. What I liked about this book is the unique recipes I found in the book and in the bonus books. Recipes like...Molasses Orange Barbecue Sauce, Watermelon Barbecue Sauce, Raspberry Chicken Wings, Caribbean-Style Rub, Spicy Cajun Rub, and Mexican BBQ Sauce.

Starting a Catering Business by Michael Rasmussen. Have you ever wanted to start your own BBQ catering business or just a regular catering business? Then this book is what you want. The Starting a Catering Business Start-Up Guide Kit is a step-by-step guide that provides a collection of valuable, sound advice and practical guidance for starting your own successful catering business.

Other titles available in our online store at www.bbq-book.biz...

Foods of the Southland – If it's down-to-earth goodness you are looking for, then this is the cookbook for you. Coming to you with over seventy years' experience. Every kitchen master from newlyweds to grandmothers from the North, South, East, West, and all over the world, should treat themselves to the greatness of Southern Cooking. Written by Dave Franks—Alex Haley's chef for many years.

Confessions of a Butcher – This book is simply amazing and is worth many, many times the small price you will pay for your instant download eBook. John tells it all in his eBook. You learn all the dirty little secrets butchers use to squeeze the most money out of their unsuspecting customers. Not only do you learn all their "merchandising" secrets, you learn all about every cut of meat imaginable. Nothing is left out.

Note: Go to our store at www.bbq-book.biz for great BBQ tools, dual probe remote thermometers, LED clip-on lights, Cookshack Fast Eddy smokers, and more!